HIS
CHURCH

HIS CHURCH

Reuben H. Mueller

ABINGDON PRESS

Nashville — New York

HIS CHURCH

Copyright © 1966 by Abingdon Press

Library of Congress Catalog Card Number: 66-28025

Scripture quotations unless otherwise noted are from the
Revised Standard Version of the Bible, copyrighted 1946
and 1952 by the Division of Christian Education, National Council of Churches, and are used by permission.

Scripture quotations noted NEB are from The New
English Bible, New Testament. © the Delegates of the
Oxford University Press and the Syndics of the Cam-
bridge University Press 1961. Reprinted by permission.

The chapter "One Body, One Spirit" is from *In the Unity
of the Faith* (Philadelphia: The Christian Education
Press, 1960) and is used by permission of the United
Church Press.

SET UP, PRINTED, AND BOUND BY THE
PARTHENON   PRESS,   AT   NASHVILLE,
TENNESSEE, UNITED STATES OF AMERICA

INTRODUCTION

This is a book whose forceful impact will be further enhanced if the introduction says something about the author. The themes of this stimulating series of essays are close to the heart of current discussion among thoughtful church leaders, and the writer is speaking from personal experience as a statesman of the church. Bishop Mueller has woven into these pages the reflections of a lifetime of leadership in posts of high responsibility in his own denomination and in the ecumenical movement.

It is not given to every leading churchman, who bears his witness through the complex and demanding channels of ecclesiastical organization, to keep his vision as clearly focused on the essentials of the gospel as Bishop Mueller has been able to do. It is even rare for a man with such responsibilities to find the time and exercise the necessary discipline to reduce his convictions to writing in a form for publication.

This book is a down-to-earth testimonial of basic conviction by a man who knows whereof he speaks. His thinking keeps close to the grass roots, to which his concern is always directed; but he illumines the local and the personal by his understanding of the global and the societal. After a period of high school teaching and sixteen years in local pastorates, interspersed with college teaching, Reuben H. Mueller was made a conference superintendent, then general secretary for Christian Education and Evangelism of the Evangelical Church. He was instrumental in the merger which created the Evangelical United Brethren Church, of which he became executive secretary for Christian Education and associate secretary for Evangelism. He was elected a bishop of the Evangelical United Brethren Church in 1954 and has been president of its Board of Bishops for a number of years.

Ecumenically, Bishop Mueller has played an important role for many years. He was long a leading figure in the International Council of Religious Education and the General Commission of Army and Navy Chaplains, of which he was chairman. He has held high office in the National Council of Churches since its organization in 1950, and in 1963 was elected to a three-year term as its president. He is chairman of the Board of Management, World Council of Christian Education and a member of the World Council of Churches' Central Committee.

Against this background the reader of *His Church* cannot help listening to the author with special respect and benefit. He will find in the very titles of the chapters some of the central themes of contemporary Christianity. He will sense the deep commitment of Bishop Mueller to the unity, renewal, and mission of the universal church. He will be struck with the perspective that has made of the writer a Christian statesman of worldwide reputation.

But while Bishop Mueller is a man of the middle way who avoids extremism in both theology and action, he is a man of courageous conviction who declares his position without equivocation. In his three years as president of the National Council of Churches he has traveled and spoken unceasingly in the name of Christ and "his church." The very selection of this title for his book is indicative of his central concern. He wants the members of all Christian churches, laity and clergy alike, "all in each place" to sense the central importance of their life and witness right where they are, wherever God has placed them in *his* church.

The book makes the basic point that this local loyalty, while fundamental, is short of the will of God if it fails to give conscious expression to the wholeness of the body of Christ, the church universal. Thus Bishop Mueller speaks directly, even personally, to the individual man and woman in every congregation, but he lifts each individual to the larger sense of identification with the worldwide community of believers. He blends the challenge of personal responsibility with the inspiration of membership in a Christian fellowship that transcends denomination, nation, race, theology, political viewpoint, economic status, and historical changes.

To every thoughtful church member who yearns to feel more keenly the significance of his local obedience in relation to the plan of Christ for his church throughout the ages and across the nations, this book will bring illumination and challenge. It should be carefully read by all who desire to grow in spirit and in truth, into a larger knowledge of the love of God for all his children.

R. H. EDWIN ESPY, General Secretary
The National Council of the Churches of
Christ in the U.S.A.

CONTENTS

11

CONTENTS

1
HIS CHURCH

The scriptural inspiration for consideration of this theme —his church—is in the words that Jesus Christ spoke to the intimate group of his disciples at Caesarea Philippi: "On this rock I will build my church." In that sentence let us pay attention to a short word, an adjective of two letters—"my." He said, "I will build *my* church." Accent and underscore that word. It is *his* church. It does not belong to man.

No man ever dreamed up the church, or laid out its plan on an architect's drawing board, or carried out the building of it. The church was born in the mind and heart of God before the beginning of time. The grand plan was laid out on the trestle board of the ages. The great architect of the universe is the architect and builder of the church of Jesus Christ. It is *his* church!

Much of the problem with reference to understanding the church and much of the basis of controversy about the church in our time can be laid directly to a misconception of the nature and character of the church of Jesus Christ. Many difficulties would be solved if we could come together in understanding the spiritual nature of the living church of Christ.

Among most people today the church is regarded as just another social unit developed by man—another social service agency to be followed or ignored. Think of a fraternal organization or a sorority, a noonday luncheon club, a musical appreciation society, an ethical culture club, a labor union, a political party, a manufacturer's association, or one hundred and one similar agencies. These are not listed to indict them. We have learned long ago that they can be good or not according to the men and women who control and use them. They are all human in their origins; they are worldly; as soon as they were born, death was already at work in them. Sooner or later they will all pass away.

But the true church of Jesus Christ is not like these. It was not begun by man; it is not manipulated by men; it will never die. It defies classification with all man-made institutions and agencies. It does not belong to Martin Luther or Zwingli, John Calvin or John Knox, John Wesley or George Fox, George Whitefield or any one of hundreds of such spiritual leaders who lifted up neglected and often forgotten truths and emphases for a new emphasis in the life of the total church. Each made his constructive contribution to the total life of the church of Jesus Christ, but it is likely that if these worthies of the faith could appear today, they would be the first to state that they laid no claims to private possession of the church but devoutly believed that the church belongs to Jesus Christ.

For many years one great segment of the Christian

14

movement has taught that when Jesus spoke these words, "On this rock I will build my church," at Caesarea Philippi, he spoke them particularly to one man—Simon Peter. And in so doing, he appointed Peter to be his successor upon the earth, and every successor to Peter at the head of the see of Rome has become the authoritative leader of the whole church.

Other segments of Christianity do not accept this teaching, not because the Roman Catholic Church adheres to it—which would be prejudice and therefore the poorest reason for holding it—but because it does not seem to make common sense. Everything authoritative and authentic that we know about Peter is all found in the New Testament. Read it for yourself in the Gospels, the book of the Acts, Peter's letters, and in several references that the apostle Paul makes to him in his letters. There are no authentic source materials besides these. Whole libraries could be filled with books that have been written about Peter, but in every case the authors are dependent upon these same source materials found in the New Testament, which is open also to us.

For example, Lloyd Douglas wrote that most interesting novel called *The Big Fisherman,* but that thick volume has in it about 99 and 44/100 percent imagination. The rest came from the authentic source book—the New Testament.

Reading about Simon Peter in the New Testament, one might suddenly remember what James wrote in his general letter. The Scriptures are like a mirror; when you look into them, you discover your own image reflected. This is true when one reads about Peter. He might find

15

himself saying, "Here is a man whose enthusiasm over-flows, but who often speaks before he thinks. Well, that describes me. I see a man who often is very impetuous in his actions and decisions. That describes me. I discover a man whose mouth is full of big promises: 'Lord, if they all forsake you, I will never leave you. I will even die with you.' That reminds me of myself. And then I discover that following this pledge, Peter has denied his Lord three times before the rooster crowed the next morning. That describes me." We are all spiritual kinfolk to this man. We are not finding fault with him or ridiculing him. We are just acknowledging our spiritual relationship; we belong to the same human family with all of its weaknesses. When we think of this, common sense says, "How can anyone—even Jesus Christ himself—build a church that is to endure forever on foundation material like Simon Peter and the rest of us. No, Peter is not the foundation of the church.

When the Reformers came, they taught that Rome was wrong at this point. It was claimed that when Jesus spoke these words to that group of disciples at Caesarea Philippi, he declared that he would build the church on Simon Peter's testimony or witness. Some of us have heard this teaching all our lives in sermons, church school lessons, and lectures: "The church is built on Peter's confession."

We still say unhesitatingly: "I cannot accept that any more than I can accept Rome's teaching for the same basic reason. It doesn't make common sense." We are not finding fault with the Reformers; we are disagreeing with the way the teachings of Luther, Calvin, Knox, and the others are usually interpreted. Those who have been in touch with Christian churches in many lands know that there are large segments of people that know nothing more about the meaning of the church than that they gave intellectual consent to a creedal statement and were baptized. No living encounter with the living Christ has ever worked a transformation in their lives, and theirs is a powerless, inactive, passive adherence to intellectual formularies.

Words in themselves do not change people, but words are constantly changing in meaning. New interpretations are always necessary from age to age. Great historic councils of churches have met in weeks and months of debate to come to agreement by the use of words with new meanings to describe old basic truths. Mere statements of belief—confessions or witnesses—are not stable or reliable enough to serve as foundations upon which the eternal church of Christ can be built.

It was not Simon Peter's words in themselves, but the truth about which he was bearing witness, that is the rock upon which the living church is built. It was not the words, limited in their meanings, but that One about whom the words were spoken that laid the foundation upon which the church of Christ is built. The apostle Paul wrote, "For no other foundation can anyone lay than that which is laid, which is Jesus Christ." Jesus is the rock upon which he is building his own church—not Peter. Christ is the foundation! And we, when we are changed and transformed by divine grace from dead building material into living stones, become not the foundation, but part of the superstructure of the church.

In the next place, the superstructure partakes of the

17

2 /

character or quality of the foundation upon which it stands. In the language of the second chapter of Ephesians they are *bonded* together. The stone that the builders rejected has become the head of the corner, but the rest of Christ's believers are built upon that foundation. I preached in the beautiful and magnificent chapel at the United States Air Force Academy in Colorado Springs. It was a thrilling experience to face 1,500 cadets in that beautiful sanctuary and to have the privilege to preach the gospel of Christ to them. The chapel is wonderful beyond description, in spite of what some architects have said about it. On that occasion, I said that this marvelous sanctuary, with its breathtaking beauty, is worth only as much as the foundation stones on which it stands. That very night, the chaplain took me down into the second basement and showed me several crumbling foundation stones. These things go together. The superstructure and the foundation are one!

This is particularly true of the church of Jesus Christ. Those who are built into his church become one in him. This means that there is only one church. There never has been more than one church. There never will be more than one church—the church that he is building, his living body, of which he is the head and which is indwelt and empowered by his living presence.

Paul writes about the church as the body of Christ. Christ is the head of this body, and his living spirit indwells and quickens this body. Writing to the Corinthians, Paul says that in one body there are many members and various organs, each one playing its assigned part. It is not proper for the hand to say to the foot, "I don't need you in my business," nor for the eye to say to the ear, "I can get along without you." Not only should each part play its individual function, but all should so cooperate and coordinate in unity and helpfulness so that they contribute to the growth and health of one another. As Paul wrote to the Ephesians in the fourth chapter of the letter, this working in harmony is for the maturing of all, until they grow up into him who is the head, even Jesus Christ. This is the purpose of the church.

Applied in a more modern sense, it is as though Paul would write that it is not proper for Methodists to find fault with Presbyterians; nor for Lutherans to refuse to cooperate with Episcopalians; nor for the Baptists to throw verbal brickbats at the United Church of Christ. These and other communions like them are not the whole church; they are manifestations in the stream of Christian history, making their contributions to the total life of the church and helping one another to Christian understanding and maturity in Christ.

All too often, religious controversy leads to misunderstanding and division, rather than the "unity of the Spirit in the bond of peace." Too much religious debate in our day is based on the desire to have one's own way at any price.

Dr. Merton S. Rice, who served for many years as pastor of Metropolitan Methodist Church in Detroit, used to tell about an elderly Quaker lady who attended his services frequently because her own church was across the city and attendance there required two bus changes. When the weather became inclement and as she became more infirm, she attended Metropolitan Church with more frequency. One Sunday morning when she was there again, she said to Dr. Rice at the door: "Pastor, you know, I've been thinking that I cannot afford to support two churches, and it is getting more and more difficult to go to my own church. I like it here. I get so much from these services. May I join your church?" Without a moment's hesitation, Dr. Rice said, "Of course, mother, you can join our church." Before he could say more, she straightened up, threw back her head to look up into his face, and with eyes flashing, asked: "Do I have to be baptized?" Dr. Rice said he could almost see a whole line of Quaker ancestors standing back of her, asking that question. He reminded us of the Quaker position on water baptism, a position worthy of deep respect; but he also called attention to our own practice and to the required question addressed to candidates for church membership: "Have you received Christian baptism? If not, are you willing to be baptized?" "Those are good and important questions for us," Dr. Rice said, "but here was a wonderful Christian woman, whom we all knew for her fine Christian witness and life. What could I say to her and not hurt her?" As he hesitated a moment, he said there flashed into his memory something he had learned in grammar school: that every good rule has at least one exception to prove that it is a good rule. So he followed that suggestion and said to the Quaker woman: "No, mother, you don't have to be baptized." "Well, then baptize me!" she replied.

Much of what goes for religious fervor and enthusiasm these days is, in the final analysis, nothing more than a desire to have one's own personal way. This causes division, and controversy, and misunderstanding when true Christian experience and action express themselves in the "unity of the Spirit in the bond of peace."

This one church which Jesus Christ is building on the rock will live forever. It is the only organism or agency among men that has the promise of immortality resting on it. Jesus promised that the church will never die. In the King James Version, it is translated, "The gates of hell shall not prevail against it." The 1901 American Standard Version reads, "The gates of Hades shall not prevail against it." The 1946 Revised Standard Version states, "The powers of death shall not prevail against it." The 1961 New English Bible reads, "The forces of death shall never overpower it." It is evident that all of these agree. Whether we say "the gates of hell," "the gates of Hades," "the power of death," or "the forces of death," they all add up to the same thing: The Church will never die! This is the promise of Jesus Christ to whom the church belongs. When time shall be no more and eternity rolls on, the church of the living Christ will be living on in his presence. This can be said of no other institution in human history. For instance, the United States government is among the very few oldest continuous governments in existence. Even our government is young, as history measures time. Governments do not last forever. Neither do any other man-made institutions or agencies. Only the church—and this does not mean buildings or man-made organizational structures, but only the living church of Jesus Christ will live forever!

Speaking to some church groups, one might ask, "Do you believe that?" It might happen that some brave

21

soul would say "Amen" out loud. This would mean consent or an affirmative vote. It may be expressed in different ways: "Amen," "I agree," "I am for that," "I vote for that," "So mote it be." They all mean that same thing. One might then have to say, "Why don't you live like it then? Get your chins up; get the spring back into your steps; get your arms swinging; let's have some action!" The church is not dead. God has not abdicated. Jesus Christ has promised victory. We are on the winning side. In the pattern prayer, he taught his followers to pray, "Thy kingdom come, thy will be done, on earth as it is in heaven."

During one Lenten season, I spoke at the downtown union service in South Bend, Indiana, at the First Presbyterian Church. There was a large attendance. Following the service, the Ministers' Association met at a luncheon in a nearby hotel, where I was guest. When the President of the Ministers' Association arose to take charge of a brief program, he began with these words: "Fellows, wasn't it wonderful to hear once again a man who believes the Church will live, that it is not dying?"

Finally, the church of Jesus Christ, which is his body, in which he lives and which he empowers and directs; the church which is one in him, and the church that will live forever—this church has the only power that can cure the hurts and ills of the world! This is the power of the keys. Jesus promised: "Whatever you lock up or imprison on earth will stay imprisoned for all time to come; and what you set free will stay free, not just for a century or a millenium, but for all eternity." Only the church has been given this power. This is the power of the keys.

There have been many interpretations of these keys. Some of them were depicted by medieval artists with medieval imagery. Search for the meaning of this imagery, and you can find nothing more significant than the report of the beginnings of the church on the Day of Pentecost, when the living power of the Holy Spirit made vital the acts of God in Jesus Christ. There began that day the imprisonment of the things that hurt, mar, defile, destroy, and kill—superstition, ignorance, hatred, sin and all its fruits. These are the enemies of man, and these are to be conquered. The power to overcome them has been delegated to the church of Jesus Christ. This includes also the power to liberate and set free: understanding, light, truth, and all that is pure, good, and holy; freedom, liberty, and especially salvation; for if the Son makes you free, you will be free indeed."

This is the promise, and this is the hope for humanity through the church of Christ. Our ultimate hope is not in missiles for outer space or treaties signed by governments controlled by men that have no faith in God and whose word is therefore not to be trusted. We ought to cooperate in every constructive movement that has as its goal the lifting of mankind into the freedom that God has promised to those who do his will. But the fulfillment of this promise can come only through Jesus Christ.

We of the church must seek our solutions to life's problems, in all of the interrelationships of daily living, in being Christian first and always, for if we really belong to his church, we have at our disposal his wisdom and his power to bring the help and salvation that is so sorely needed in the world. Remember, it is *his* church!

2

SERVANTS OF CHRIST

Many incidents in our immediate past have made us feel that each year could be called a year of crisis. Internationally there is the ferment of shifting policies and new alignments. The worldwide movement of the dispossessed toward freedom, self-expression, and self-determination has focused itself nationally upon the drive of Negro Americans toward full participation as citizens in a democracy. The United States Congress has struggled for financial integrity. On the moral and religious fronts serious questions have been asked about America's future in these areas and, therefore, in all her life.

A prominent magazine assessed our moral situation by declaring that three institutions of our American life have a tremendous responsibility for influencing morality: government, business (including labor unions), and the church. It declared that all three have failed.

November 22, 1963, burst upon us with shocking and shaking horror. We seemed to think it could not happen here. In Kenya, the Congo, Venezuela, Viet Nam, Cuba, the Dominican Republic, Haiti—yes, but not here. Yet it did! President Kennedy, champion of civil rights for all people everywhere, became the victim of hatred gone mad. Fanatical and bigoted agitators could attack the integrity of our institutions and our leadership and trigger the "mad dog" acts of those who seek to take the law into their own hands and become the executioners of those who do not agree with them. What our times need most is the particular demonstration of our faith that is different because it dares to be Christlike!

A portion of one of the servant songs of Isaiah is most appropriate as we face the future. In the intuitive insights of this poetry we are brought face to face with the tremendous challenge of the Suffering Servant of God to become servants of the living Christ.

Isaiah 53:12 declares: "Therefore I will divide him a portion with the great, and he shall divide the spoil with the strong; because he poured out his soul to death, and was numbered with the transgressors; yet he bore the sin of many, and made intercession for the transgressors." This is a summary evaluation of the servant of God against the background of the description that has preceded it. This is the portrayal of the kind of servant who can acceptably serve God and his cause. This is quite different from present-day job descriptions that set forth qualifications for government service, industrial positions, or other intergroup or international representations. It also seems inconsistent with the standards set by the records of historians, who list and describe the "great ones"—such as Alfred, Peter, and Richard—Charles, Wilhelm, Catherine, Ivan, Peter, and Frederick—and so on. When the word "great" is used in the teaching of history in our secular schools, it has a significance altogether different from the way the word is used in Isaiah.

For here is the description of abject defeat, of mistreatment and abuse and suffering when viewed merely from the human point of view. But this is the paradox that our Christian sources always set against the background of the usual patterns of the rest of the world. One dramatist caught it up in the words, "She stoops to conquer." But more plainly and clearly, if we would win, we must first know what it means to lose. If we would be leaders, we must first learn how to follow. If we would rule, we must first learn how to obey. If we would be great, we must first serve. If we would live, we must first be willing to die. Hear the greatest teacher of them all when he says: "Whoever would be great among you must be your servant." His day did not understand this, nor does our day yet comprehend it. But this is the pattern that is presented to us as his followers, and we must follow this pattern if we would be servants of the living Christ.

Many different answers have been given through the years concerning the identity of the suffering servant referred to in Isaiah. We read that some suggested Moses, some Jeremiah, others Isaiah himself—and still others, the entire nation of Israel. But in spite of whoever may have been the prototype, the Christian church has always been sure that these servant passages came to real fulfillment only in Jesus of Nazareth. To me, it is most revealing to discover in the book of Acts that this kind of interpretation brought dramatic spiritual results.

You will recall that a government official from Ethiopia was on the return trip from Jerusalem when he picked up a hitchhiking Christian layman along the Gaza highway. The account has it that this ambassador had become interested in the Jewish scriptures, and now, in true oriental fashion, he was reading aloud from the scroll of the prophet Isaiah as his chariot rolled along. Also in like fashion, the layman (named Philip) spoke into the reading, asking: "Do you understand what you are reading?" This elicited an invitation to mount the chariot and to interpret the reading. The passage that he was reading was this: "As a sheep led to the slaughter, or a lamb before its shearer is dumb, so he opens not his mouth." (Acts 8:32.) And then follows the striking observation: "Then Philip opened his mouth, and beginning with this scripture he told him the good news of Jesus." And the record states that the ambassador believed and put himself on record publicly as a follower of Jesus Christ. This is the acid test of experience. Jesus Christ, as the suffering servant of Jehovah, blazes the trail, and if any would be servants of the eternal Christ, they must follow in this way.

Now, try to apply this paradoxical spiritual principle to our responsibilities as servants of Christ in our mid-twentieth century world. There is a guarantee here that obedience to this principle will lead to a place of greatness (as God measures greatness) and will make it possible to share in the results of victory. The abject and pitiable, humiliated and abused man who hung upon the cross of crucifixion has become the most significant personality of all history. Jean Paul Richter said that with Jesus' pierced hands he had lifted empires off their hinges and turned the stream of centuries back into its channel. And Lecky too, the historian-philosopher, said that the three short years of the public ministry of Jesus had done more to soften and regenerate mankind than all the disquisitions of all the philosophers and all the exhortations of all the moralists since the world began. This strange and powerful personality promises sharing in his kingdom to all who are strong enough and daring enough to pay the price. That price is to be found in the right kind of response to the conditions that Jesus Christ himself met when he gave his life in order that he might take it again and share it with all who would follow him. It seems to me to be wrapped up in one summary word: "because." And there are four causes briefly:

I

"Because he poured out his soul to death." This is the challenge to *dedication*—to complete and unreserved self-giving. It was his response. It has been the response of every man since that time who has achieved greatness in service to humankind in the name of Christ. The heart of this is self-sacrifice. But this does not necessarily always mean physical death. The requirement here is to be willing to give everything for a cause, even to the very point of giving life itself. Sometimes physical death might be the easiest way to die. There are scores of deaths far more significant than that. And until one is ready to die to some things he will never do much in the area of race relations, ecumenicity, the establishment of peace, or in achieving economic justice for all. This is true in all of life's relationships and experience. For example, take the area of music. In Chicago quite a number of years ago the world's

leading concert pianist appeared in Orchestra Hall. All seats were sold out, and the "standing room only" sign had been taken down. The audience of music lovers sat entranced as the master musician brought forth from the treasure store of his training, experience, and gifts in music interpretations of the masters that thrilled all who listened. Then came the intermission, and as the people relaxed and moved about, some visited. In a gallery section sat two men, who discussed what they had heard and experienced. Said one of them: "I wonder how long a man would have to practice before he could play like that?" His neighbor replied: "Well, I have just read a story of his life, and he himself said that it was twenty-eight years before he was allowed to appear on a first-class concert program." Think of it! Twenty-eight years getting ready to be Paderewski! Twenty-eight years of elementary instruction, of tedious and monotonous practice, of hours on end of slavery to the instrument and to the laws of music, while others were enjoying life's freedoms! And this sacrifice had not even ended at that time, for Paderewski said that unless he rehearsed hours on end each day, his artistry immediately suffered.

But this is true not only in music. It is a principle for all of life. In our modern day we do not seem to have the patience for this. One could go even further and say that such devotion (used in the Old Testament sacrificial sense) is fading too much from us. Ralph Parlette used to say to his school lecture course audiences that we Americans want to do everything by way of the shortcut. We would become educated by taking six lessons with a correspondence school. And then, in his characteristic fashion he would add: "You can grow a mushroom in one night, with the accent on the mush, or a pumpkin in one season, with the accent on the punk. But when God grows an oak tree that can be turned into beams to bear the loads of commerce in shipping vessels or on bridges, it takes years of battling the elements to develop strength."

Here is a lesson for us as churches. We render distinctive and meaningful Christian service when we are willing to die, if necessary, to further the Christian cause. And it is always necessary! But this is not the way of the institutions and organizations of the world. Therefore, if we insist on handicapping ourselves by using the methods used by those who do not know Christ, if we do not have a "plus element" in our being and doing that is distinctively Christlike, then we can expect only the kind of results any other agency could produce. This would make the church wholly unnecessary. It is this principle—"unto death"—that ought to make the service of the church different. The suffering servant attitude in church worship involves this willingness to surrender sovereignty for the sake of a redemptive purpose, to find life more abundantly through dying to self and to institutional vested interests. It may become necessary for denominations to die in order to advance the cause of Christ in this world in our time. It has been said that when the World Council of Churches will really have done its work well in guiding the unity of the church in Christ, then it will have put itself out of business. This is our first challenge! "Because he poured out his soul to death."

II

There is a second reason. *"Because* he was numbered with the transgressors." This is the challenge to *identification.* Another great prophet like Isaiah put it like this: "I sat where they sat." The suffering servant counted himself one with those who were condemned under the law. This is the essence of his redemptive self-giving for all of mankind. For us, as we follow him, it means identification with all who are victims of the injustices and inhumanities that man inflicts on his fellow man. There is no area in the present time where this is as significant and important as it is in the area of human and civil rights, for these affect the race problem. Until, as Christians, we can identify with the people of other races, we will never find the correct and abiding solution for this problem.

Take the case of the Negro in America. The advancement of America's colored people in many respects has been amazingly slow. For decades Negro groups have petitioned the whites for relief from injustices with so little success that the Negro has now lost faith in this method. In the Niagara Declaration of Principles in 1905 there were five chief petitions: (1) The right to vote; (2) the end of discrimination in public accommodations; (3) the right of free association with any man; (4) equal enforcement of laws; (5) adequate education. None of these goals has yet been fully realized in the United States. Many appeals have preceded and followed the formulation of this statement, but as far as Negroes can observe, they are largely disregarded. Moral and spiritual appeals do not seem to move "Christian" white America. The one hundred years since the Emancipation Proclamation have been filled with disillusionment on both the national and personal level. And now the Negro has decided that he must pursue a plan of action based on his own observation and evaluation of the American scene. He senses that the basic factor is materialistic. A threat to profit or property can seem to move a white Protestant a lot faster than an appeal to "spiritual" ideals. An economic boycott or a bit of destructive civil disorder seem to bring the white people to the conference table ready to bargain in good faith faster than any other method. Also, someone has observed that most Americans respect the successful man, no matter what his means of success. Therefore, since the Ten Commandments are not the absolute for most men any more, the Negro senses that he must have another power base. The methods of the Revolution of 1963 were based largely on such considerations. The Negro believes that if he stands up like a modern man, the white man must accept him. Now, if we want to understand that, we must put ourselves in his place. We must identify with him in his concerns for his family and his own future—with his problems, aspirations, and suffering.

Thank God there is a growing, conscious effort among our churches to do just that! It is but a beginning, like "a cloud the size of a man's hand," but please God, it shall grow into a mighty, driving force. Beginning with the action of the National Council's General Board in 1963, when the Commission on Religion and Race was created and activated, the churches have addressed themselves to the critical situation in race relations in a manner unparalleled in history. The Council has given itself to the awakening of the churches to action—to go beyond theorizing to demonstrating.

Under this impulse there was strong representation of our churches in the unforgettable march on Washington on August 28, 1963. In a manner far beyond the dreams of friend or foe there was demonstrated that day, for the benefit of all to see and heed, the concern of the churches for the cause of civil and human rights of all people. Elemental justice demands that this cause be prosecuted until Americans of all races, creeds, or conditions are granted first-class citizenship.

But there is something even more significant than justice involved here for the Christian. Because he is a committed follower of Jesus Christ, he must give expression to the concern of Christ for the oppressed, the dispossessed, the enslaved, the downtrodden, the underprivileged everywhere in the world—for did not Christ say that he came to fulfill Isaiah's words:

The Spirit of the Lord is upon me,
because he has anointed me to preach good news to the poor.
He has sent me to proclaim release to the captives
and recovering of sight to the blind,
to set at liberty those who are oppressed,
to proclaim the acceptable year of the Lord (Luke 4:18-19).

III

There is a third reason. *Because* "he bore the sin of many." This is the challenge to *compassion*. It follows identification but goes deeper than identification. It not only expresses sympathy for those who suffer from the ills that afflict our humanity, but it is willing to enter into

33

the fellowship of this suffering. In a real sense, this is the essence of the oneness of the church. The phrase "all in each place one" takes on tremendous significance when we begin to "bear one another's burdens, and so fulfil the law of Christ." As Jesus put it to his disciples, "for you have one teacher, and you are all brethren." Our unity depends not so much upon ourselves as upon him and our relationships to him. It is this that establishes our right relationship to one another and establishes it so that nothing can separate us from the love of Christ or from each other.

It is this that brings us to share in a sense of guilt over the burdens and oppressions and persecutions of all the peoples of the earth. It is this that brings to us a sense of sympathy or pity for all who suffer without cause because of the inhumanity of man to man. It is this that helps us to understand why the peoples of Africa and Asia and the islands of the Southeast have as much right to "life, liberty, and the pursuit of happiness" as we have.

Perhaps we can communicate this best by means of an experience that Mrs. Mueller and I had in the city of Berlin in 1961. Responsibility for the supervision of our own communion in Germany and Switzerland takes me to Europe from time to time. On this particular occasion I was presiding over our East Germany Conference, most of which is behind the Iron Curtain. Under present governmental restrictions our ministers and lay delegates from our churches outside West Berlin were unable to come into that city for the sessions. Consequently they met in Dresden and then came to East Berlin in order to confer with me. A code telegram had been sent across, stating:

"Onkel wird Abendmahl feiern." ("Uncle wishes to celebrate communion."). Once we had been cleared through Checkpoint Charlie by United States military guards and by the East German police and had been met by our superintendent, who took us to the church where the consultation was to occur, we gathered in fellowship first at the Lord's table. I have shared in communion in many churches and places around the world, but this one was different—moving and convicting and wall-shattering— where strong men wept as they received Christian communion in spite of the wall. For its shadow was there.

We recalled that the superintendent had not ventured to come close to the checkpoint lest the police check on him. His car was hidden one and a half blocks away behind ruins, so his license number could not be traced when it might be observed that he picked up foreigners. In the conversation of that day we learned of the intensification of "refined" forms of persecution these people were experiencing, such as their youth being compelled to choose between their Christian faith and fellowship or losing their jobs and their livelihood. Before that day's consultation came to a close, I asked the superintendent privately whether any one of his pastors might need to be moved into free Germany to save him or his family from the rigors of persecution and the threat of breakdowns. Without hesitation he said to me, "Bishop, every man of us has pledged to stay at his post, come what may. It is our firm conviction that if our people ever needed pastoral care and counsel and the assurance that the church cares, that time is now. We are staying!"

He said this without any attempt at bravado, no sign

of playacting, no false standard—simply, quietly, but firmly and deliberately, "We are staying!" Identified with their people to the utmost degree of carrying their burdens with them, these people have caught the deeper meaning of compassion.

But this has haunted me. Back here in America in our privileged and affluent society, and in our urbane religious self-satisfaction, I have been caught asking myself, "Could you find an equal number of men here who, under similar circumstances, would respond in the same way?" I am not saying that I could not. I do not know what similar circumstances might produce among us. God knows! But I think I do know that a religion that cannot stand that test is not good enough for these times. It makes no difference how logical or theological dissertations may be, not how learned and erudite our theories of interpretation, not how skillfully we can analyze and debate the issues of social responsibility—all of which have their place. The real question is do we really have the kind of faith and dedication to the will of God and the way of Christ, that will stand this acid test?

IV

There is a fourth and final reason for our servitude under Christ: *Because* he "made intercession for the transgressors." Without question this underscores *intercession*. It is the logical—sometimes even the chronological—consequence of these other reasons for greatness and victory. This is heard again from the parched lips of the Son of God on the cross: "Father, forgive them; for they know not what they do." Dedication, identification, compassion, and now, intercession. This means far more than a few pious verbalisms, even when couched in the language of prayer. Here again, it is basically a matter of the whole life of the servant being thrown into the act of intercession for another, even for transgressors. This is the essence of evangelism—the kind of evangelism that will lead to the renewal of the church. It is both personal and social.

In the words of Alan Walker of Australia, "Personal and social witness belong together in evangelism. Personal evangelism by itself is largely irrelevant in our world; on the other hand, social agitation which has lost touch with its evangelical base is a waste of time."

A news report of that South African mission carries these striking sentences:

Clergymen were thrilled to see their people commit their lives to Christ, to see signs of renewal of the church achieved because the church had done what it was meant to do: move out into the world with the gospel. They recognized afresh what "the whole gospel for the whole world" really means; it crystallized their thoughts and galvanized them into action. As one thoughtful man put it: "This mission means that we go on from Galilee to Jerusalem, from the quiet place of popularity to the unquiet action of putting the challenge of the gospel at the heart of the nation's life, with all that means in terms of danger, even of death. But this is the way the Master went."

This is the way we need to go here in America too. As servants of the living Christ we need to be dedicated to the servant's way. It is a way marked by bleeding footprints.

3

"RENEW MY CHURCH"

In that time-tested literary epic *Quo Vadis,* the author
made a lasting impression on readers' minds with this
question, "Whither goest thou?" The early Christian
martyrs answered this question with dauntless courage
in the gladiators' arena or in the lions' pit. The Roman
political despots thought they could stamp out this strange
Galilean cult that released a mysterious power into human lives and their interrelationships by means of non-
violent witnessing. This little handful of Christians not
only determined the direction of their own movement,
but also the trends of civilization for several centuries to
come. In three hundred years they quietly penetrated the
Mediterranean world with this new way of life made possible through living relationship with and through Jesus
Christ, their risen Lord. Eventually even the emperor
was enamored and intrigued by this remarkable movement.

However, when Constantine professed to embrace the
Christian faith, about A.D. 320, for political purposes he
made baptized "Christians" en masse, often at the point

of the sword or the spear. Because of this the clear direction of the Christian movement was corrupted by its marriage to the political and military power of empire. Nothing worse could have happened to it for that immediate time and for the centuries that followed. Down to the present day we suffer from the blight and the curse of this adulteration. We see evidences of this on overseas mission fields where there is confusion between sharing the Christian gospel and sharing the ideas and methods of Western civilization or culture. We also see it here in America today, where many otherwise sincere and well-meaning people are being duped into following a self-appointed religious power-structure that is more bent on promoting a self-indulgent political and economic system, supported by the religion of the status quo, than it is on mediating the spirit of the living Christ to all people everywhere.

There never was a day in our own generation, when this question was more pertinent. *Quo vadis?* Where are you going? Or to make it more American, where are you heading? No question could be more challenging today. Nothing could be more basic or important than to ask ourselves, where to now? From the point of view of a churchman, what does it mean to find the Christian answer to *Quo vadis?*

In 1938, the annual session of the International Council of Religious Education, the forerunner of the Division of Christian Education of the National Council of Churches, was being held in Chicago. In a pastors' advisory section that was studying the values of applied psychology and psychiatry in relation to pastoral services, the guest speaker and resource leader was Dr. David Seabury of New York City. He had held attention as he elucidated his theme, referring frequently to the "protoplasmic drive," and its effect on developing life. He spoke in most favorable terms of the necessity for a close relationship between religion and the psychological practitioner. When he opened up the period for questioning, one of those who responded to his invitation asked, "Granted the significance and importance of all that you have said, just where does God, or faith in God through Jesus Christ, enter into that which you seek to do to cure people? You have not mentioned God once in your presentation." To this question Dr. Seabury gave a very wise and helpful answer. He had taken for granted since he was speaking to a group of Christian ministers that we understood that God is in the entire process. He is the author and sustainer of life. He is concerned about the well-being of people more than anyone else can be concerned. Without him, and the proper reverence for the lives he creates and loves, no one can really help people. He went on to say, "The work that you pastors do is far more significant than what we psychiatrists can do. If people would really accept the message of Christ and center their lives in him, most of them would find the solution to their problems and therefore would not need the specialist in psychology."

That raises the question, "Do we take too much for granted in religion?" If we do assume the spiritual bases in life's experiences, wouldn't you think that once in a while the evidences of the religious or the spiritual would manifest themselves in life? The greatest teacher who ever lived and taught said, "You will know them by their fruits."

The first thing to say about the direction in which we are going is that we must demonstrate more than theological theories and/or ecclesiastical or ecclesiological organization and administration, if we would affect the nature and quality of human living in these times. This is not said by one who tries to sit in judgment on other peoples' spiritual claims; we are merely stating that our day is saying to all of us in the field of religion: "Put up, or shut up." It is just as plain and challenging as that. Ivory tower meditations have their times and places. Mounts of transfiguration are tremendously important for inspiration and for building inner resources to meet the down-to-earth demands of the valleys of life.

A young nobleman in ancient Israel gave himself with enthusiastic devotion to a political reform movement that was sadly needed under the conditions of those times. He had become a follower of the king who seemed to hold promise for a new day of righteousness. But when King Uzziah died suddenly and the reformation collapsed, a disillusioned Isaiah turned to religion in desperation. How human! In the temple, seeking divine help, he experienced a vision of God Most High and confessed his responsibility and guilt in the society of which he was a part. Then he experienced the cleansing of conscience and heart that gave him new courage and responded to the call of the Eternal by giving himself to help his people find themselves in the right relationship to God. In this experience there is a spiritual "plus something" which he received and which he shared with the people who responded to his mission.

It is this "plus something" that we are concerned with here. The burning embers on the altar, the insistent call of the hour, the sense of the divine presence—however it is put into words—we could use a lot of this in our time. We have a great deal more of it among us today than most people are aware of and some are willing to acknowledge. We must not castigate people for shortcomings and failures for which they are not basically responsible. Instead, we ought to seek constructively to encourage Christians to behave as followers of Jesus Christ ought to behave.

This could raise the question: How do we get beyond what has become to many people (according to the way they express it), "a fervent faith in a very vague religion." The Marxist would carry this much further and aver that this is a basic characteristic of religion: an opiate to keep the people quiet, satisfied, and submissive under any outward conditions. Or, to take yet another tack, how do we answer our theological friends from Europe who accuse American churchmen of being too activistic in the expression of our religious faith? Amid the resulting confusion, compounded by yet other factors, for me a living faith in God must manifest itself in human interrelationships.

From a Judeo-Christian point of view, we are our brother's keeper in a very true sense. Jesus emphasized this in the parable of the Good Samaritan. And in his public ministry, from the day he announced his purposes in his maiden sermon, he dedicated himself to the purpose expressed in Isaiah 61:1 and 2. Every one of these has social implications.

This means that a John Wesley of the Church of England could not only recover the spiritual worth and significance of the individual, but that this concern could lead directly to facing the circumstances created by the dawning of the industrial revolution, as they affected the coal miners and mill workers of England and Wales. Walter Rauschenbusch's emphasis was not only on the social implications of the gospel, much as that was needed for the day, but he was concerned that Christ-owned persons should express this concern in doing something concrete about the social problems men created for themselves. Therefore, we need to dig deeper, to understand better our own spiritual heritage, in order to participate more effectively in the Christian programs that seek the correct solutions to our common problems and to enter into the ecumenical conversations and procedures going on round about us.

This raises some questions for most people: Should we get more deeply involved in the social, economic, and political problems of the day? Of the nation? Of the world? There are good, sincere, and pious people who say this is none of religion's business. They are prone to become very vocal in repeating criticisms of the National Council of Churches that are prepared and distributed by printed page and soundwaves by men and organizations whose religion is pugnacious and narrow. This kind not only makes the National Council of Churches its favorite whipping boy, but practices Hitler's theory of the "big lie": If you tell it often enough and loud enough, the common people will begin to believe it! This is how Nazi Germany was born. And this is how religious fascism is at work in the United States today. Everywhere in this country people are saying: "These accusations must be so, for no one representing the Council gives answer to those criticisms and charges." So the faultfinding continues, spreading half-truths and untruths; maligning men and women of good Christian character; condemning the member denominations of the Council for entering into cooperative studies and producing findings and making recommendations of how Christians ought at act toward these matters in our present-day world.

However, let us be not nearly so concerned with the professional religious baiter, faultfinder, and iconoclast, who is forever blindly smashing his hammer against everything outside his own program, as we are with the good, sincere people who have been led to become critical of the social application of the gospel through the definite efforts of the churches. One wonders how such people read Amos and Hosea, Isaiah, Jeremiah and Ezekiel, and how they have missed the fact of Jesus' own declaration of his purposes as he went about *doing* good, not just *talking* it.

If Christians and Jews are to become more deeply involved in the kinds of problems we have mentioned, then how do we go about making our views heard in the areas of race, ethics, civil rights, automation, labor-management relations, and government and help create a Christian public opinion? How can we bring the positive influences of Christian faith to bear effectively on the circumstances and conditions of our society without losing the unique spiritual contribution that religious people ought to be making to their times? There are other problems too, such as: Does religion have anything to say relative to the modern population explosion? Or to the fact of rural decline and urban increase? Or to the continuing problems of ethical and moral standards and practices?

We have raised far more questions than we can possibly answer. There is no pat, cut-and-dried answer that fits every problem. We deal with life and its ever-changing circumstances, and static solutions are not possible. But one thing must be said because it is basic. The religious person—the man of faith in God, and for me, especially the follower of Jesus Christ—cannot face his problems and try to solve them in the same way and by the same means that nonreligious and antireligious people do. This does not mean that he must be against those means and methods. Let us take for granted that they are morally and ethically sound means. But, in addition, they ought to be spiritually sound, and the man of religious faith and conviction ought to do more than expound this truth; he ought to expose it in the manner of his living. This is the kind of power that needs release into our society; that lights up the way for others by *being* as well as *talking*.

The temptation is to try to use nonspiritual methods to enforce spiritual ends or goals. The largest effort ever devised along this line in our lifetime was legal prohibition. By surrender of a good principle to the methods of unprincipled politicians, havoc was made of ethical and moral standards for many people. The aftereffects are with us yet.

To illustrate in another way, the city of Indianapolis

was stirred up some time ago over the Sunday closing question. Efforts were made by the Church Federation and many churches to seek legal protection for Sunday. The best results came, however, from an appeal to the sense of responsibility for others and for conscience' sake that persuaded some businesses to support Sunday closing. But today such gains have all been lost. Indianapolis is wide open on this score to the extent that the main downtown merchandisers have joined the practice in their shopping center outlets. And no one is raising much of a protest over this development. The merchants are members of churches too, and the explanation given, when you ask them, is that the public demands this. If we are to judge by what happens at one of the shopping centers, we should have to say that the largest group that shops on Sunday is the group that has just come from the worship services at nearby churches. Of course, the fourth commandment is only one out of ten; and for many people, in our enlightened day, relativity has modified the meaning of most of the ten for most people. The real question is not: How can I enforce these rules for right living on others? but: How do *I* measure up? How real is religious truth for *me?* What do *I* have worth sharing with others of spiritual faith that would help solve the problems of the times?

In religious circles and conferences, there is a deepening concern along this very line. There seems to be welling up a widespread hunger for spiritual reality and spiritual renewal. It was heard and talked about at New Delhi at the Third Assembly of the World Council of Churches. Hardly a religious gathering of any consequence is held without reference to it. Pope John XXIII made this a chief burden of his call for the Second Vatican Council. It was in Philadelphia at the Triennial Assembly of the National Council of Churches that guidance was sought from the message of God's suffering servant. This kind of renewal is not made by man. It is a gift from God that cannot be earned or merited. It can just be received. But this implies a willingness to be committed wholly to its meaning.

When Francis of Assisi prayed in the little tumbledown Chapel of St. Damien, he said that he received a commission from Christ, as though he heard the words: "Renew my church." In the zeal of this experience, born in prayer, this dedicated monk went about the task to restore the chapel. He begged and borrowed, and when funds were obtainable, he bought stone and wood and other materials to rebuild the chapel. But it did not take long until he discovered that it could never happen that way in his whole lifetime. What was needed, he came to sense, was a complete dedication of himself, involving long nights in prayer vigil on the mountainside, until the whole community was convinced of his dedication. Then the replacing of rotting timbers and fallen doorsills lost its significance because of what was happening in the lives of people. The real church was being renewed.

It seems that the time is ripe for such spiritual renewal to give rise and impetus to a new spiritual advance. With the terrific problems facing our times and a world in the throes of change everywhere, we face anew the tremendous question: "Where are you going?" Are we seeking a day, scientifically oriented, with affluence as its goal and independent of God and his claims on his children, ending like atheistic and communistic Russia on the scrap heap of civilization? Or will we be wise enough to give spiritual values their rightful place in our daily living, so that we become practitioners of God's way of life and not mere theorists of it?

4

"ONE BODY, ONE SPIRIT"

Our theme and subject arise from the study of the *church* epistle, Paul's letter to the Ephesians. In the fourth chapter Paul reaches the high concept of the unity of the church and lifts high the challenge of the "unity of the Spirit in the bond of peace." "There is one body and one Spirit," he writes. Why then are there so many different, and differing, churches in the world? Why so many divergencies in doctrine and such sharp contradictions in practice among those who call themselves Christian? In the United States alone our Census Bureau has reported more than three hundred different church bodies. On the worldwide scene over two hundred churches belong to the World Council of Churches at the present time. For many of these groups there are explanations in historical and national backgrounds, but for many others there is no other excuse for existence than the spirit of disunity and human divisiveness. In more recent times the trend seems to be toward unity of purpose and endeavor, and we see a growing cooperation among most Christian bodies in our day. Gradually but steadily it seems to be dawning upon the leadership of our churches that Jesus Christ cannot divide himself—that his own body, the church, must be one. *The followers of Christ ought to be together.*

Some years ago the leadership in overseas missionary work came face to face with the fact that our denominational differences have little meaning for new converts in new mission lands. They discovered that our many divisions into denominational groups worked to confuse the Christian movement. The creation of the International Missionary Council was a strong effort to minimize these differences and to develop increasing areas of Christian cooperation. Through the leadership of Christian statesmen like John R. Mott and William Temple (to name just two), study and consultation conferences were organized and carried on in the areas of Christian life and work, and Christian faith and order. Eventually, under the impact of the tragedy of a worldwide war, it was decided to bring into being a cooperative organization whereby the churches of Christ could come together in Christian unity and bring to the world Christ's healing and saving power. In Amsterdam, Holland, in 1948, the World Council of Churches was launched, into which fellowship were invited all Christian communions who confess "Jesus Christ as divine Lord and Savior." In this never-to-be-forgotten meeting in Amsterdam, communions frankly faced their differences but discovered that they were together in Jesus Christ and therefore confidently heralded to all the world: "We intend to stay together." In their next world assembly at Evanston, Illinois, in 1954, they reviewed the progress that had been made, evaluated their

continuing problems, and announced just as confidently:
"We intend to go forward together."

Thus the whole Christian world has been alerted to
the movement toward Christian unity, but at the same
time it has been made aware of the things that have
divided Christ's followers in the past and often still create
divisions today. It is very important to recognize and
to realize that the frank facing of our differences is the
first step to understanding and appreciation. We are learning that unity does not necessarily mean conformity—not
even uniformity.

In facing up to these facts we want very much that our
people understand that we are not advocating a thought-
less easygoing and shallow acceptance of everything that
is written and spoken these days under the subject of
ecumenicity. Much is being written and said on that subject, and much of it concerns itself with the protection
and conservation of traditions and practices and verbalized
beliefs, as well as of rights and privileges of organizations
and persons in ecclesiastical structures and positions. Perhaps this all has its place in the scheme of human progress,
but there is one important and basic factor in this matter
that is often neglected and too much overlooked. It is
basic to the solution and understanding of the whole
problem—namely, the Spirit. Paul says that "there is one
body and *one Spirit*" in the church of Christ. Too many
people seem to be concerned chiefly with the "body" and
give major attention to the structure and organization
for unity. There is no question in my mind that the Spirit
requires incarnation in a body, which is the church; but
reaching even further back into this analogy, we find that

51

the Spirit is much more significant than the physical body.

At the Conference on Faith and Order held in 1958, in Oberlin, Ohio, the main theme for consideration was: The nature of the unity that we seek in the church. It was most encouraging to sense that there the major concern was with this "unity of the Spirit," more than in schemes of organic union. There were representatives present who were promoting different schemes of organic union, but the voting body of the conference turned these down for consideration and declared that our chief concerns must be with the attitudes and convictions and spirit of those who are responsible for guiding our churches toward the goal of Christian unity.

In harmony with this, the "unity of the Spirit" depends more upon our encounter with Jesus Christ and our relationship to him, than it does on our wisdom or achievements or positions. This is what our Master prayed about in his high priestly prayer in the Upper Room when he prayed the Father that "they may all be one." It is what Jesus declared to his disciples, when he instructed them about proper attitudes among his followers. He said, "For you have one teacher, and you are all brethren." To sharpen this meaning for ourselves, we could well say, "*Because* Christ is our Master, *therefore* we are all brethren."

This fellowship depends not so much on what *we* know or plan or achieve, not upon *our* positions or honors or attainments, but upon *him* and our relationship by faith to *him*. The important thing is not who *we* are, or to what group *we* belong, or how much *we* have accumulated by way of honors or distinction or material wealth—but *who he* is, and what our relationship is to *him* and to everything that *he* came to do and is doing through his body, the church. We need to take our eyes off ourselves and look to him; take our eyes off the fragmented expressions of his church, found in our divisions, and look to his unified body; take our eyes off of our circumscribed understanding and look to his revelation of the purposes of God. We need to learn that our doctrines, as statements of our human interpretations, are less important than the living truth which they try to imprison in creedal formulas. For in its deeper sense, Christianity is not so much a body of doctrine as the living relationship between persons. God is not so much one about whom we are to think and philosophize as one with whom we have to do. True Christianity and true Christian faith move in living relationships. These include our relationships to God and to man through Jesus Christ. This unity that is in Jesus Christ is the real basis of our togetherness and points up the basic relationship to God through Christ in the forgiveness of our sins and the acceptance into the fellowship of Christ. This transcends statements of theological faith and recognizes the fact that there must be diversities in expression of such beliefs—because no one man can develop a perfect and complete theology from his limited experience and viewpoint. Therefore, the spiritual relationship and attitude are far more important than anything else, and the development of such a fellowship, graced by Christian charity, is our great need. Furthermore, when this fellowship is realized, the things that tend to separate us and keep us apart lose their power, and we are drawn to one

53

another in Christ, by his Spirit. This is true Christian ecumenicity.

This is all more easily stated than practiced or experienced. There are so many things, not of his Spirit, that work to keep Christ's followers apart. When one applies this Christian truth to the chief tension points in our own times, one begins to see how frustrating and vexing, and yet how necessary, this is. In theory, this sounds trite and worn by repetition. But whenever we dare move from theory to practice, we come face to face with a tremendously revolutionary principle for life. It is the kind of revolution our world needs.

Let us try to apply this principle to the three chief tension areas of our times.

I

There is, first of all *the area of race relations,* in which tensions have been increasing all over the world. Everyone seems to have heard about America's concerns with the racial issue, and many are highly critical of how America is trying to solve this problem that came to us many years ago when English and Dutch slave ships raided the African coast and brought the Africans, under compulsion, and sold them in America to the cotton growers. How can the descendants of these people live together in the same communities as neighbors today?

When my wife and I arrived in Nigeria in Africa in the winter of 1957, to visit our daughter and her family who were in missionary service there, we met the native African manager of the United Africa Company among the first ones who greeted us. He was a keenly intelligent and capable businessman, entrusted with great responsibility for this inland trading post on the Benue River. After the formal greetings were over, the first thing he said to me was: "Now tell me about Little Rock." And he had a right to know. So I told him about Little Rock and the shame and disgrace of a state governor's action; and about narrow and bigoted people who will sell out the education of their own children for a mess of pottage. But I also told him about the teen-age Methodist high-school student who stood up in a crowd of her fellow students and openly declared that it was not Christian to deny the colored youth an equal opportunity for an education with the white youth of her community. One wonders why the newspapers of Europe, Russia, and Asia have not been as keen about reporting this event, as they were the disgraceful conduct of the politicians of that community.

It would be possible to recite the story of many of our communities that have written a record for history in which the minority group and the persons of races of another color have had their civil rights and liberties protected and guaranteed. In this respect, we in this country are no different from the decent and good people in many other lands who believe in the rights of man, for most countries have their race problems and their minority groups. But the fact remains that only in those countries where the Christian gospel has been proclaimed and has developed principles and ideals of righteousness and liberty, have men secured liberty for themselves and their fellow men.

Men will learn how to live together as brothers when

they have become the children of God through Jesus Christ. Whenever their lives are changed and transformed by the power of the redeeming indwelling Christ and they have become a part of the life of his body, the church, there will be no race distinctions to separate men and keep them apart from others. Jesus Christ makes us one even across racial boundaries. This is easier stated than practiced. But it is our need.

In Nigeria, one Sunday morning, as we sat in the native church service among some five hundred black worshippers, I noticed that the man in front of me bore on his body the marks of a leper: the white spots on his elbows and legs, the stumps of fingers. He was not lovely to look at. But as I looked, suddenly I realized that this man was worshiping; he is a Christian believer; he is a member of the church of Christ. He belongs to the body of Christ. And, so do I. Therefore we must belong together in that body. And this we do! And the hope for our future in this world in these relationships between men and their races depends on Christ's people realizing this and living it.

II

In the next place, there can be only "one body, one Spirit" *in the area of relationship between churches or communions,* if the tensions there are to be resolved. Dozens of illustrations could be marshalled from our many church groups in the United States and the sorry spectacle they set before the world with their strife and competition—this in the face of the words of Jesus when he said: "I do not pray for these only, but also for those

56

who are to believe in me through their word, that they may all be one; even as thou, Father, art in me, and I in thee, that they also may be in us, so that the world may believe that thou hast sent me" (John 17:20-21). The unity the church has in Christ is to be the witness to the world that Jesus Christ is the Saviour sent by God.

But here again, this is not confined to our country. In the summer of 1958, in Okinawa, the so-called missionaries of dozens of denominational organizations were overrunning that island and causing consternation among the Okinawan Christians because of the unchristian competition and divisions among these missionaries.

And in Europe, of which we outlanders are learning more and more in these recent years, the relationships between many churches are best described as a polite respectability, dictated by the untoward circumstances of wartimes and postwar circumstances. Think how long the leadership of the established churches harried and tried to suppress the free churches and similar movements, and in how many places the word "sect" is still pronounced with a scornful curl of the lip!

And so, all over the world, the unbrotherly spirit manifested toward one another by many who call themselves followers of Jesus Christ is one of the greatest hindrances to the progress of the gospel that we know anything about. One of our outstanding American preachers, in a former generation, called this "the scandal of modern Christianity." Of this we need to be cleansed, and it can happen only through the Spirit of our Lord Jesus Christ bringing us into a unity of the Spirit that transcends the disunities of words, doctrines, customs, prejudices, and pride. Often it seems that some of us are more concerned about "disputing about words to no purpose." This does not mean that thought and debate and discussions in matters of doctrine or theology are unimportant, but it is possible to reason and argue and debate about the thirteen major theories of the atonement, for example, without ever having experienced for oneself the glorious experience of "at-one-ment" with Jesus Christ through his redeeming grace. To grant to others the right to sincerity in positions they hold, even though we cannot subscribe wholly to those positions, seems to be part of that true spirit of Christlikeness that Paul wrote about to the Corinthians: "Now I know in part." To confess frankly, that at our best, we cannot imprison all the truth in our little human definitions, and that others may have an understanding of certain facets of truth that we have not yet experienced, seems to be the only Christian way to consider one another's statements of belief or creed. To recognize frankly our honest differences and to learn to appreciate one another's contributions to the truth that is in Christ seem to be of the Spirit of Christ and a strong evidence of our unity in him. This Spirit the Christian witness must recover if we are to have influence and power for God in the world. Thank God that there are some evidences in our time that this is slowly coming to pass.

III

Finally, there should be only "one body and one Spirit" *in the area of international relationships.* This is the third great tension area of our modern lives. The entire world is divided into two warring, scheming camps: East versus

West. The western nations fear the Russian and Chinese coalition, with their satellite slave nations and their godless philosophies based on naked power. And the eastern powers fear the West which has possessed ruling power in the world for a long time and has left some ugly blotches on the pages of history to prove how human, and sometimes how near the beast, they too are. Distrust and fear rule the interrelationships among the nations of the earth. Cold war and an uneasy peace haunt both our waking and our sleeping hours. Who of us, on either side, does not fear what a day may bring forth?

Thinking of all this and much more that is related to it, we come at last to remind ourselves that God's word has promised that "the kingdom of the world has become the kingdom of our Lord and of his Christ, and he shall reign for ever and ever." For God has not abdicated his throne. Jesus Christ is still Savior and Lord and the Prince of Peace! And he shall one day put all kingdoms under his feet and reign as King of kings and Lord of lords, forever and ever.

In this lies the only hope of the world; not in so-called statesmen who do not honor or fear God, and to whom the moral commandments are myth and legend, and whose word, therefore, cannot be trusted, even when signed with pomp and majesty in formal ceremonies. Nor does the only hope of the world lie in the piling up of atomic armaments that have within them the Frankensteinian power to annihilate civilization, nor in the economic oppression of the underprivileged peoples by the more favored nations, even when the latter are motivated by paternalism.

But our hope is in Christ, by whose indwelling Spirit

we come into oneness of spirit with him and thus with one another. This is the magnificent obsession of those who believe in Jesus Christ as Savior and Lord. And these are the true "peacemakers," whom Jesus called "blessed" and said they would be known as the "sons of God."

In Berlin, following the closing session of the East Germany Conference in 1956, one of the Evangelical United Brethren chaplains in the United States Army took us out to his headquarters and into the chapel, where I preached at the vesper service. Present in the service were some of our U.S. military personnel and their families and some of the German civilians who were employed on the Army post. I spoke on "Blessed are the peacemakers," and in the course of my message paid my respects to the war-makers of the past—the so-called heroes of the battle-fields. I called some of them the "butchers" of the nations. By way of contrast, I held up the Prince of Peace as our leader.

Following the service, there was a coffee hour in the social room, and during this period I suddenly found myself in a corner of the room, with a cup of hot coffee in one hand and a doughnut in the other and a German matron standing in front of me, cutting off any escape. Then, shaking a finger in my face she said: "Nun, Herr Pfarrer, was machen Sie denn mit unseren Helden?" (Now then, Reverend, what are you doing with our heroes, anyway?) She was greatly incensed that I dared to speak as I had about these heroes of the battlefields. She informed me that it was essential to use the stories of their heroic deeds to develop these virtues in the children. Patiently I heard her out and then said to her: "My dear woman. Here you stand defending the very system that has destroyed Germany. As for me, away with your war heroes, and ours too. I have a greater hero than all of them. He never shed any blood but his own upon the cross, and he did that for others. He did not come to take life but to give it. He is the Prince of Peace, and I am his follower. This is why I want to be a peacemaker and not a warmonger."

I have often thought since of that experience. How many people are there who follow blindly, just as that woman did, the power philosophy of the jungle? And what chance will we ever have to bring this old world to enduring peace until professing, believing Christians leave their superstitions about politics and international relationships, and begin to let the light of Jesus Christ shine into these dark places in the world?

I am one who believes that it is beginning to shine in our times through Christian men of influence and stature, who are standing true to Christian ideals and are doing their utmost to preserve peace with honor in our time. We pray for them daily. We preach hope even in this dark international hour. "For what we preach is not ourselves, but Jesus Christ as Lord, with ourselves as your servants for Jesus' sake. For it is God who said, 'Let light shine out of darkness,' who has shone in our hearts to give the light of the knowledge of the glory of God in the face of Christ" (II Cor. 4:5-6).

5

"ALL IN EACH PLACE ONE"

The year before the Third Assembly of the World Council of Churches met in New Delhi, in 1961, its central committee held a very important meeting at St. Andrews in Scotland. Some people go to St. Andrews to attempt its difficult golf course, but these World Council of Churches men and women were there to examine the basic purpose and program of the World Council in preparation for the World Assembly. Probably the most significant declaration that came out of that St. Andrews' meeting was that the ecumenical movement is altogether too much a special class movement. It includes in its adherents so-called top ecclesiastical and theological leaders of denominations and communions around the world, but these leaders are not very well known, and much less understood, at the grass roots of the church—in local communities and parishes. The time had come, the committee agreed, when this movement, if it was to be significant in our times, would have to penetrate the entire church and enlist the understanding and loyalty of the rank and file of the church's membership. Out of these considerations the members coined this striking phrase: "All in each place one." That is, the followers of Jesus Christ must recognize their unity in Christ in the local communities where they live and work, and in those same communities they must practice Christian brotherhood and cooperative Christian service, as they seek together to fulfill the world mission of his church.

It is reported that the Faith and Order Conference at Montreal, in 1963, was even more explicit, going so far as throwing aside the preconference agenda and insisting that this is the basic problem for us in our time.

This means that ecumenicity is not just something for world assemblies of churches to talk about, or for national assemblies to hear addresses about. It is something that is important for state councils of churches too, and county and city councils of churches. More than that, it is basically important for every Christian church and for every believer who puts confidence in Christ's command to go into all the world with his mission. It is not something exclusive for a select group who are so initiated and esoteric that some have dubbed them "ecumaniacs." I do not believe that the values and blessings of the truth that is in Christ are so hedged about with mystery that only a few religious Einsteins can grasp them. Christian truth and Christian experience are for everybody, everywhere, and at all times. This means Europe and the Near East and the Americas and the Australian continent, but it means the Far East and Africa and the Southeast Islands, too. This means Philadelphia, Baltimore, New York, Geneva, and London, but it also means Tokyo, Moscow, Cairo, and Durban. It means the white man and the brown man and the yellow man, but it means the black man too. It not only means mission work in Japan and India and the Congo, but it also means the Christian mission in East Harlem, Chicago's south side, and Indianapolis. In fact, it includes the place where you live!

Too few people in our churches know about the significance of ecumenicity, or even understand the meaning of the word "ecumenical." This is true, in spite of the fact that dictionaries are available almost everywhere. Ecumenical means "the inhabited earth"—world wide in extent, influence, and significance, and when applied to the church, it implies inclusion of the whole church in the whole world. After all, when you come to think of it, there were relatively few people who had the privilege of attending the New Delhi assembly where this was carefully discussed. And attendance at the Philadelphia assembly was relatively limited also. There are a great many people in our churches, and I mean local or parish churches, who have a very limited, and sometimes incorrect, notion of what ecumenicity really is.

In 1957, Dr. Henry Pitney Van Dusen was speaking to a World Mission Institute in Evanston, Illinois, and dealt with this kind of a situation relative to the understanding of ecumenicity. He said in part:

It is a truism of ecumenical history that advance in Christian unity in almost every aspect has gone forward, faster, and farther at the world level than at the national level. On the other hand, it is a dogma of democratic doctrine that any sound development should originate at the "grass roots," and work upward thence, toward national and global expression. Neither world nor national ecumenicity can be healthy or secure unless and until it is grounded upon local ecumenicity. One often hears it said that sooner or later Christian unity must achieve "grass rootage." I believe that the time is now. . . .

If this is to take place, two major revolutions are required: on the one hand, in the conviction of church leaders that it is important; and on the other hand, in the understanding and leadership of Christian unity in local communities. . . . The pretension of national or world Christian unity, while Christians and churches in local communities continue in unreconstructed division and separation, is insincere as well as unreal.

But what is this "grass rootage" to which he refers? As usually understood, it means an effort to make congregations aware of national and world ecumenical developments. Now, this *is* important, and a great deal of progress in understanding has been achieved in this respect. But true "grass-roots ecumenicity" implies something far more drastic and more difficult—namely, the achieving of functioning Christian cooperation and unification in local communities. This demands a radical change of focus in most places. It means turning the direction of effort and devotion in a united way to the local scene and, consequently, finding the ablest leadership for councils of churches that can be found.

This has special significance for the conciliar movement. This means (if we really mean it) that the council of churches should be the powerhouse of united spiritual, evangelistic, Christian educational, and social action advance for all of the churches of the community. And this means also that its executive director and other leaders should be the ablest and most trusted influential persons in the Christian forces of the community. It is stated in this form because here is a place where every one of us can make a direct and significant contribution to the realization of Christian unity right where we live and work. This is the ecumenical imperative for these times. It confronts us with the challenge of St. Andrews: "All in each place one."

We have tried to say that the need for understanding and practice of ecumenical Christianity is on the local level. But how is it usually understood there now?

Dr. John D. Ickes of the Bronx Council of Churches in New York gave several graphic illustrations of this understanding, in a thought-provoking article in *The Christian Century* not long ago. He cited three illustrations:

1. In one suburban community, a denominational board of home missions organizes a congregation, buys ground, and builds a chapel. Its name: "Blankville Community Church," plus (in parentheses) the name of the sponsoring denominational body. This is illustrative of the growing tendency to de-emphasize denominationalism in order to facilitate the crossing of denominational lines by prospective members. Is this what we mean by ecumenical Christianity.

2. Councils of churches in many cities sponsor various types of interdenominational services at certain times of the year, such as the Easter service, or Reformation Sunday, or summertime park Sunday evening services. These are given "all-out" publicity so that large numbers often attend and thus participate in a united witness. Dr. Ickes asks if this is ecumenicity?

3. In thousands of communities, councils of church women sponsor interchurch worship and in a united movement help worthwhile causes by working on service projects. At times their united worship takes the form of Holy Communion, since they are not inhibited by theological formulas. Is this ecumenicity?

To these examples from Dr. Ickes, could be added another list: preaching mission programs, community visitation evangelism projects, national Christian teaching missions, united ministries to migrants and to wartime defense communities, and many others. Today, one must not fail to add civil rights demonstrations that seek to awaken community and national consciences to the right of all men to equal opportunities and to first-class citizenship.

Now, we are not impugning all or any one of these movements. There are many good and constructive things that could be said about them, and again and again, they have produced good Christian results when carried on by people who were properly motivated and related. We know that they grow out of Christian motivation, and we know that by and large they do manifest united Christian witness and action. But at best, these are only piecemeal.

The real meaning of the worldwide, all-inclusive Christian movement is to be found deeper than in any one of these surface manifestations. It is to be found basically in spiritual relationship to Jesus Christ and therefore to our brothers and sisters in the church. No one has stated this more succinctly and clearly than Bishop Lesslie Newbigin of the Church of South India. "The language

of our Lord's prayer [in John 17, that his followers
might all be one]," he says, "points to a unity which
is not merely analogous to the unity of the divine
nature . . . but actually a participation in the being of the
triune God. . . . The unity which we must seek is thus a
unity which arises from Christ's indwelling in his people,
and from their being in him. It is not simply a unity in organization, nor is it simply an agreement about doctrine.
It is a total mutual interchange of being—Christ wholly
given to us, we wholly given to him. This is a unity involving the whole being of all concerned in it. It is not
of the same kind as any other human unity. Its pre-
condition is the forgiveness of sins—God's forgiveness of
us, and our mutual forgiveness of one another. Its character is not simply described by saying that those participate in it who love one another as Christ loved them. This
means that the question of agreement on doctrine . . . is
essential to unity. Our participation in Christ depends
on our hearing, believing, and accepting in common,
the message of God's saving acts in him. Without this
basic consensus of belief there can be no unity. But the
unity in question is not in essence an intellectual agreement about doctrine: it is a total mutual reconciliation
which is the result of being born anew by the Spirit. It is
a unity of mutual love given by God. This unity is com-
patible with a wide variety of form and emphasis in the
statement of doctrine. The variety of doctrinal formulation
of the New Testament testifies to this. No one finite
mind is capable of achieving a complete and perfect men-
tal formulation of Christian doctrine. It is only by the
interplay of differing human insights within the bonds

of divine charity that an adequate testimony is given to the fulness of the truth as it is in Jesus."

In these striking thoughts Bishop Newbigin has elaborated that which the apostle Paul wrote to the Ephesian Christians concerning the "unity of the Spirit in the bond of peace." It is tremendously important that we understand that this is a spiritual unity.

In the next place this kind of unity is a primary objective of the conciliar movement. It seeks, first of all, not organic union nor monolithic oneness, but spiritual togetherness. That there will be trends toward actual organic union between denominations, as they become better acquainted with one another, no one can deny, and many of us would encourage. This is especially true of churches of the same confessional family, or with the same historic backgrounds and similar beliefs and practices. But it does not require organic union to be in the unity of the Spirit and to demonstrate the oneness in Christ in witness and in action.

This is strongly illustrated in the relationships of councils of churches on the various levels of action. The fact is that there is no necessary organic or structural relationship between a local council of churches and a state council, or between state councils and the National Council of Churches; or between the National Councils of Churches and the World Council of Churches. Membership in those various councils is by denomination and not by council organization. But in spite of this fact there is a spiritual relationship that unites them in the ecumenical Christian movement. It is a matter of goodwill, of fellowship in Christ, of common faith and ideals, and therefore of spiritual unity. These councils are the churches in united action on the various levels, but that which motivates this united action should be the spiritual oneness that centers in Jesus Christ. When this is present, even interdenominational cooperation becomes not only a possibility, but a reality, without any disloyalty to the denomination.

This is something of what Patriarch Athenagoras had in mind when he supported the quest for Christian unity. He insisted that he was not speaking of theological unity but rather of a unity that would have two aims. "In its negative sense it would disarm hatred, distrust, and bad propaganda between church groups. In its positive sense, such unity would promote contacts between these groups on the common principles of Christianity and how they should be propagated."

In addition, this ecumenical spirit, this unity in Christ, is more than an ethereal idea or a strange religious feeling. It manifests itself in life, in action, in bringing God's resources to bear upon the problems of our human existence and interrelationships. It is not some private experience to be enjoyed and stored up just for ourselves. If we really know Christ; if we have become unified by the Spirit in his body which is the church, then we will be called to take our knowledge and our experience into the world for which Christ died. There are those in our day who object to the church, or the church's ministers (whether lay or clergy) having anything to say or anything to do with life's issues in politics, in industry, in civil rights, in international relationships. They say, "Let the church be the church and stick to religion. Let it be spiritual." This is a corollary to Karl Marx's teaching, that religion is the opiate of the people. Either way, the intent is for religion to put the people to sleep so they will docilely submit to those who oppress them. One wonders what kind of answers Amos or Hosea or Isaiah or Jeremiah would have given them. We do know that when Jesus started his public ministry, he took the text for his maiden sermon from Isaiah's declaration of social responsibilities and declared: "Today this scripture has been fulfilled in your hearing."

This leads us to ask, how can we, in our time, follow him in such application of our lives out into the world for which Jesus Christ gave himself? How can this need be fulfilled in us? How should Christ's people behave in the face of civil rights problems, integration barriers, religious misunderstandings, and international fears and hatreds? There is no smooth answer for these rough problems. We only know that we must try, but that in that trying we must stay close to Christ. We cannot do these things correctly by ourselves.

In the visit that five of us—Mr. J. Irwin Miller, Dr. Eugene Carson Blake, Bishop B. Julian Smith, Dr. Robert W. Spike, and myself—made to the President of the United States on December 9, 1963, at his invitation, we were prepared for our audience with the President in the Justice Department offices by the assistant and deputy attorneys general. During this lunch period we heard from a member of that staff who had served on a case in Mississippi. It was a sordid story of the bestiality and inhumanity that the responsible leaders of a community there wreaked upon helpless women in jail, whose only offense was that they had plead for decent treatment for their fellow men. They had been manhandled and beaten and bruised by other inmates of the jail, men who were made

71

drunken by the jailor and then ordered to do the dirty work. One can hardly believe that civilized man in our so-called Christian society could stoop so low. The women were seeking redress and justice under law. Physicians exhibited photos of their bruises and swollen backs and limbs; the men in jail who had been the dupes who perpetrated the horrors admitted their part under duress on the witness stand. In spite of this, leading church members of the community mounted that same witness stand and, under oath, denied all charges and testified to the good character of those who were responsible for these abuses. The case was in the hands of the jury for but a brief time, and the verdict was "not guilty." The federal government, through the Justice Department could do nothing for justice in the face of this community. As we talked about this later on as we drove to the airport, Mr. J. Irwin Miller said, "But one thing is certain, it seems to me. These people will have to live with their consciences. Deep down in their hearts they know they lied and committed wrongs against fellow human beings. They will never be able to escape from that. And that will one day bear its fruit." This, I too believe! When enough of us believe this, there will be united action that will change our communities and our times, not by the spirit of hatred, but by the Spirit of Christ.

One other illustration. Following the visit of the church delegation from Russia and other satellite countries in 1963, there was a peace conference in Prague which the superintendent of the Evangelical United Brethren Church in East Germany attended. He wrote of the joy that was his when several of these representatives who were there told him they had met me and brought him my greetings. He described their reports of their trip and said that by and large, they had glowing reports and were greatly pleased at their experiences. But there were two things that troubled them, that were hard to understand. First was the picketing to which they were rudely exposed. This to them was inexplicable. The other thing was that apparently we Americans are not interested in a Christian peace, because we do not participate in the Prague Peace Conference.

I wrote to him as a Christian brother. I told him that the pickets were an Americanism—something that we endure here, just as we have to when we go to Europe and read on the walls, "Yankee Go Home."

As for the matter of peace, I assured him that we are very much concerned about peace in our time—but a peace that comes through Jesus Christ. I am unqualifiedly opposed to the kind of peace that atheistic communism offers the world because I am absolutely opposed to atheistic and communistic principles and systems. My own church and our sister churches and our National Council of Churches have long since declared themselves openly, in print and otherwise, clearly and unmistakably against communism and its products.

But we are concerned that men of goodwill unite their witness and their service in the cause of Jesus Christ, the Prince of Peace. In this quest we will join with all men everywhere that in this area too all in each place may become one in Christ.

6

MY RESPONSIBILITY TO MY CHURCH

Some years ago, there came to my desk an attractive little tract published by Church World Press of Cleveland, Ohio, entitled, "My Threefold Obligation to My Church." No author's name was given. It was brief, pithy, straightforward, and challenging. I do not recall anything that this anonymous author wrote in his testimony, except the three main points, about which he gathered his declaration of responsibility to his church. These were: (1) I should *pray* it up; (2) I should *say* it up; and (3) I should *pay* it up. This is my threefold obligation to my church. While this is certainly not poetry, there is a certain rhythm to the accent on the words that rhyme in these three short sentences. This makes it a device to aid memory in recalling these significant words of personal witness.

I am using these three ideas as the means for conveying my own testimony about my responsibility to the church. I am not using any further words from the tract. I am sure there are many persons who were helped by reading it. Before I discuss these specific statements, however, I want to make two essential observations about this threefold testimony to show why I hold it to be so important.

First of all, the *order* is important. Prayer belongs first, testimony follows, and stewardship is the logical sequence and consequence when the first two have been faithfully practiced. This is the only safe and sound way to support the church of Jesus Christ. It must be remembered that we speak not of a church that is conceived by man's wisdom, organized by his own skills, and dedicated to doing only his will. We are considering the church for which Jesus Christ died on the cross, giving his life so that his church could come into being. "Christ loved the church and gave himself up for her." (Eph. 5:25*b*.) It is our obligation as Christians toward that church that concerns us, and that requires something far deeper and more sacrificial on our part than many of us practice as church members.

Christ also determined the order. "But seek first his kingdom and his righteousness, and all these things shall be yours as well." (Matt. 6:33.) The spiritual must come first. If we change that order, we are headed for trouble in our own spiritual experiences. This is true of individuals and of congregations. Almost every striving Christian can give personal testimony of this truth in his or her own experience. Congregations do not often see this nor practice it as they ought. How much time and energy, how much struggle with plans for raising money to pay bills, have congregations poured into their efforts because they seek first to take counsel with their fears, and by word of wisdom set their limitations on the work of Christ's church? If much prayer and thorough dedication were resorted to first as the basic essential, the financial stewardship program of many a church would be filled with blessing and victory. Prayer, testimony, stewardship—this is the correct order.

The second observation is that the *direction* is important. It must be *up,* not *down.* We are to pray the church *up;* we are to "say" the church *up;* we are to pay the church *up.* Not down! Prayer is a divinely ordained privilege given to man, whereby we use it as a spiritual lever, placed on the fulcrum of the cross of Christ to lift the church up and nearer to the heart and will of God. Christian testimony is the use of the divine gift of human speech for giving expression to our gratitude to God for the provision of our spiritual welfare through the gift of his Son Jesus Christ, and for sharing this experience with our fellow men to the praise of Jesus Christ. Such witnessing is uplifting and constructive. If the praying has been right, then the testimony will be right, for the overflow of the heart will be in life-giving terms and not in poisonous and destructive words. The direction is *up!*

And when the praying and witnessing have been right, then the paying will be right too. It will be up, and not down. Too much stewardship has been cheapened by paying a dollar down and then proceeding to ignore and evade the balance of the obligation. Instead, we ought to understand that here is an account that can only be paid *up* to stay in good standing with Christ, who gave up everything for the sake of his church.

Now, remembering these two basic considerations, let us look at the threefold statement of obligation to the church of Jesus Christ, that every member has to that church.

MY RESPONSIBILITY TO MY CHURCH

First of all, we must *pray* the church up. This is our basic obligation, our primary responsibility so far as his church is concerned. We must join multitudes of other Christian believers in a deepgoing undergirding of prayer that will lift the church closer to the heart of God.

There are those who claim to be followers of Jesus Christ who try to use prayer to pray churches down and to pull individual disciples down in the esteem of others. It is very hard to understand such spiritual ignorance and such debased attitudes when some people seem to think that their own lives are the standard of Christian perfection and that God is concerned with bringing everyone to their norm of experience and action.

While I served as a district superintendent in Indiana, there was one city in which an independent prayer band let it be known that it was committed to this kind of program. It was composed largely of people who had "fallen out" with their congregations and who had gravitated into this supercritical body that pursued the self-appointed task of purging the churches of the city. I learned about it first from the pastor of one of the Evangelical United Brethren congregations in that community. He told me that the prayer band had passed the word that it had formulated a prayer list of certain ministers of the city and had set itself to the task of asking God to remove those pastors, one by one, from the life of the community because they were considered to be "blind leaders of the blind." This pastor's name was on that list. But the man at the top of the list was the pastor of the First Congregational Church.

When, after some months of such prayer activity, the pastor of the First Congregational Church suddenly became ill and then soon died, this prayer band exulted in the fact that God had answered its prayers. And the members let it be known that they were going on with their prayer lists. However, about three months later the so-called pastor of their own church died, and they became very quiet because they had made themselves the victims of a foolish "boomerang" theology. God would not be involved in such unspiritual and unchristian prayer activities, but these misguided people had the sincere conviction that they could tell God what to do.

As a young teen-age lad in my preacher-father's congregation in Minnesota, I had an experience in prayer meeting one night that shocked me terribly in this area of Christian experience. Being the "preacher's kid" I had no option about being in prayer meeting, such as that exercised by the sons of trustees and stewards and "leading church members." So I was the lone teen-age boy, wholly undisturbed by others and thus able to give complete attention to the praying of the saints, whether I wished to or not. Consequently some of the recurring prayers—the same words, phrases, sentences, and nuances of expression —became engraved on my memory. But one evening this routine was suddenly shattered, when one of the pillars of the congregation changed his diction and his emphases and emotionally asked God to take sides with him against another man in the congregation, who was kneeling no more than twelve feet from him. I do not know what others may have felt, but I do know that that teen-age lad was electrified, shocked, stabbed wide awake by the audac-

ity of a man who claimed to be a Christian, calling on the
Eternal to take sides in a petty quarrel and drag the other
man down in the esteem of his Maker and of his fellow
men.

What is it in human nature that makes us want to pull
others down in order to make a heap upon which we think
we can climb and crow over our fellow men? More important than that, what makes any of us believe that the
eternal God can be implored by means of prayer to take
part in our petty differences and our sinful jealousies and
hatreds?

Jesus has something to say about this. He spoke one
day of two men who went up to the temple to pray, one
a Pharisee and the other a publican. The Pharisee stood
forth among other worshipers and prayed something like
this: "I thank thee, God, that I am not like the rest of
men, greedy, dishonest, adulterous; or, for that matter,
like this tax collector. I fast twice a week; I pay tithes
on all that I get." It was as if the Pharisee were inviting
God to look him over and recognize his goodness. He
wrote his own recommendation in superlative terms. He
painted the most sinful background he could think of and
then placed himself in front of it by way of contrast. To
make himself look better, he tried to tear other people
down—and with prayer.

But the other man, the publican, kept his distance,
Jesus said, and "would not even lift his eyes to heaven,
but beat his breast, saying, 'O God, be merciful to me, a
sinner.'" Calling attention to the comparison between
these two praying men, Jesus said about the latter, "I
tell you, this man went down to his house justified rather

than the other; for everyone who exalts himself will be humbled; but he who humbles himself will be exalted" (Luke 18:14). This is Jesus' evaluation.

Real prayer can never be prostituted to the devilish ends of tearing down and destroying our fellow men. Real prayer can be used only to lift up, to undergird, to bring life into right relationship with God's will through Jesus Christ our Lord. Therefore, when we pray for the church and all who are included in Christ's church, we should pray it up. This is basic. It was one of the first things Jesus Christ taught his immediate followers. He taught it both by personal example and by pattern prayer. This is the starting point; it creates the right climate spiritually for fellowship with the Father and with his Son, our Savior. Until this is established, it will not be possible to be in right relationship with our fellow men. It is prayer that binds us to him and to one another in the fellowship of his church.

Pentecost Before the day that the church was born in the stream of history, preparation had preceded it in the form of ten days of prayer, ten days of confession and forgiveness; ten days of cleansing and crucifixion of the human ego; and ten days of abandonment to the Holy Spirit's cleansing and enduing power. When the church of the Upper Room was "prayed up," and not until then, it was "dynamited out" into the world to bear witness before men and to call them to repentance and faith.

The history of those first days and years is replete with the story of prayer unlocking the resources of heaven for the redemption of men. Early in the record of Acts we read that they met constantly to pray. And again, "When they had prayed, the place in which they were gathered together was shaken; and they were all filled with the Holy Spirit and spoke the word of God with boldness" (Acts 4:31). Prison doors were shaken and opened; learned rabbis received their spiritual sight; lame men were made to leap for joy; the leader of the church had his spiritual understanding broadened as he prayed and was saved from segregated pride and selfishness; and a fellowship grew and stretched across thousands of miles, but was held together by the bands of prayer. Paul's letters are filled with expressions of prayer for others and admonitions to pray for one another. This has been true of the Christian church throughout its history. When prayer has become secondary and then has been neglected and, as a consequence, the sense of utter dependence upon God has been lost, the effectiveness of the church in human history will have waned. But whenever prayer has become the major instrument of faith and action among confessing Christians and has been restored to its primary place, there will come spiritual reformation and renewal in the life of the church and in her witness to the whole world. In my judgment, we stand in need of just such renewal today. The need is everywhere recognized. But many are busy trying to attain such a goal through restructuring church organization and program, or through rephrasing creeds and formularies and rituals. One would think that the past experience of the Church through the centuries would make us wise enough to know that

> More things are wrought by prayer
> Than this world dreams of.

81

We stand in need of a universal, thoroughgoing Upper Room prayer revival that will seek to know God's will and obey it through Jesus Christ, our Lord.

There are many more reasons for the Christian using prayer to lift the church up, in addition to those from church history. There are personal reasons, very often intimate and precious and, therefore, not talked about much but very real, nevertheless. One needs only to reflect on how often and how constantly the church has prayed for him throughout his lifetime to be moved to the prayer of gratitude. I owe it to my church to pray for it because my church has always prayed for me. Before I was born, Christian parents prayed in anticipation that God would grant them the blessing of parenthood. When I was dedicated to God in Christian baptism in my infancy, my parents and church prayed together for me. When I, of my own volition, some few years later committed myself as a confessed follower of Jesus Christ and joined the fellowship of his church, the congregation prayed for me. When I declared openly that I sensed a calling to the Christian ministry, my church prayed for me as preparation for attesting to its faith in the integrity of my call and response to it. When I was ordained to the Christian ministry, my church, by the "laying on of hands" of the elders and by the praying of the assembled Conference, set me apart for this ministry. And throughout the years of pastoral services and administrative responsibilities, I have been encouraged and helped again and again by hearing my church pray for me and my colleagues, as it lifted us on arms of prayer before the throne of God's grace.

And what shall one say about those ties when serious

illness threatened the life of a loved one or of oneself, when the church stood by in earnest intercession while life hung in the balances—or, when the messenger of death called a loved one home, and the brokenhearted ones who are left behind are comforted and solaced by the consciousness that the church cares and prays?

You see, my church has never forgotten to pray for me. Sheer thankfulness dictates that I carry on this prayer-ministry on behalf of others—multitudes of others with terrific temptations, with sorrows, and with the dangers of successes—who need the prayers just as I did, and do. God knows that we all need the lifting power of such praying. I owe it to my church that I should pray it up.

II

When we have been faithful in meeting our prayer responsibility, then we will be ready to say that we must "say" the church up. Translated into simple American idiom, this would read: "We must *talk* the church up." Here again we need to be reminded that the direction is important, as is the order. When our prayer attitude is correct because the Holy Spirit is guiding us, then our verbal witness will lift and not tear down. When the fountain source has been cleansed and sweetened by prayer, then we need not fear the import and effect of the spoken words concerning the church for which Christ gave himself.

Human speech is a gift from God. By its means we can release ideas into the lives of others that will either bless or curse them. Such a divine endowment, intended for man's good, can be abused and abased and used for devilish ends.

If so used, it is then no longer Christian in essence and purpose and has no rightful place in the life of a disciple of Christ.

In the days just prior to the Civil War, Henry Ward Beecher was pastor of the Second Presbyterian Church in Indianapolis, Indiana. It was located in the business district, and though Indianapolis was then a much smaller city than it is now, this church was experiencing an attendance that constantly ran well over four hundred each Sunday morning. The building was crowded, and this was considered an outstanding achievement. One Monday morning as Dr. Beecher was walking to the church office, he fell into step with a businessman friend, who was a prominent member of the downtown church of a sister denomination. As they walked along, the businessman asked Dr. Beecher how many had attended Second Presbyterian Church the morning before. The answer was that the head usher had reported about four hundred and fifty. After a moment's silence the man asked a question: "Dr. Beecher, how do you account for the fact that while you had four hundred and fifty present, our church was nearly half empty? I think our minister is an excellent preacher too." Under pressure from his friend, Dr. Beecher then told him what he thought about the comparison. He stated that the man's pastor was his very personal friend and that he regarded him as an outstanding preacher. Shortly after he moved to Indianapolis, he began to hear members of this man's congregation gossiping about the minister and officials of the church. He said, "If I had not been a minister and had been looking for a church home and had heard those members of your church finding so much fault with the leadership and criticizing the minister, I never would have come to your church. Over at our church, when I get up to preach on a Sunday morning, I face over four hundred persons who believe in the gospel I preach, who support me with their prayers, and who are loyal in their talk about their church throughout the week. They are the ones who tell other people about our church, and always there are people in Indianapolis who come to services to see whether it is all true, and many of these are persuaded and become a vital part of our fellowship." There was a congregation that "talked up" its church.

One of the best Bible preachers and strongest spiritual leaders of the Evangelical United Brethren Church was reared in a devout Christian home in Dayton, Ohio. He often related how Sunday dinner at his parental home was a time when there usually was "company" invited by the various members of his own large family. Theirs was a home of Christian hospitality as well as of strong Christian convictions and standards. One Sunday noon as they and their guests were gathered about the dinner table and grace had been spoken, the man of the guest-family attempted to begin the table conversation by means of critical faultfinding with the morning sermon by his preacher. At that, the head of the host-family said sternly: "Hold your tongue. In my house nobody criticizes his preacher nor finds fault with his church." That father considered it far more important to protect the formative spiritual lives of his own children than to bow to the amenities and niceties of being host. He made an impression upon his own children that endured for a lifetime. How much unfaithfulness to the church could be traced back to disloyal and unchristian tabletalk and family conversations when children were growing up and attitudes were being formed! The direction is important. *Up,* not *down!*

The prayerful, faithful constructive witnessing of the devoted members of Christ's church can do much to advance the effectiveness of that part of the church to which they belong. This does not mean the special witnessing of formalized occasions nearly as much as it means the unconscious influence of ordinary and regular conversations in all the relationships of daily life. Let us talk the church *up!*

III

Finally, when we have been faithful in meeting our prayer responsibility to the church and have borne witness in harmony with our praying, then a third thing must be done: we must *pay* the church up! This is sound spiritual logic. It follows a spiritual sequence. It is the soundest Christian stewardship program we know anything about. Meeting our financial responsibilities to the church should be the flowering of our personal relationship to Christ through prayer and the voluntary testimony of our lips to the goodness of God to us, as we try to share that with others. An old biblical proverb states, "For where your treasure is, there will your heart be also" (Matt. 6:21). There is a vital relationship between our spiritual membership in Christ's fellowship—the church—and in our honest evaluation of it through our speech about it, and in our willingness to make all of this available to others.

This is the true motive for Christian giving in and through the church.

This is not a matter of the size of one's giving as compared with the giving of others. It is much rather a matter of our giving to make possible the sharing of what Christ's church has come to mean to us in our experience, so that others can come to have similar experience. If no one else were moved to give on these terms, we should still have to give, as Christ gave himself for others. There is no escaping this. At the seaside at Caesarea Philippi that morning when Peter asked Jesus, referring to John, "What shall this man do?" Jesus answered, "What is that to you? Follow me!" Here is a responsibility that is deeply personal and one that no one can meet for us. We must meet it according to our abilities, as God has prospered us both spiritually and materially.

In the depression years of the 1920's and 1930's, in a southern Illinois countyseat town, a young man inherited a small triangular acreage without farm buildings when his father died. The small rental price that he could receive was not sufficient to make much difference in his financial resources. But his father and mother had left him something more valuable—a deep abiding faith in the goodness of God and the records of faithful witnessing to Christ all their days. This was his heritage.

To obtain work in those days was difficult for anyone. He finally leased a gasoline service station and operated it successfully enough, so that he ventured to propose marriage to the girl he loved. She was of similar religious faith and conviction, and together they set up a Christian home. One of the operating principles of this new home was that one-tenth of every dollar of income would be religiously devoted to the Lord's work through the church. Every week, after he paid his one helper, computed the tithe, and paid all of the bills, they found that they were getting along better than most couples of their acquaintanceship. They had nothing extra, but they were well taken care of.

Then one day a representative of an American oil company walked into his filling station, laid a contract or lease form on his desk, and asked him to sign it. There had been an oil strike in the Wabash River Valley, and it looked as though it were going to develop into something of considerable size. The oil companies were leasing all the land they could, and this company wanted the lease on his thirteen-acre tract of farmland, offering a nominal sum, but also the royalty rights prescribed by state law should oil be found. He signed up and forgot about it. But some months later, when a representative of this same company called to deliver a five thousand dollar check to him as the first payment on oil brought in from drilling and said there would be more from time to time, this young man did not suddenly lose his spiritual bearings as many others did at the time. He walked down to the bank, deposited the check, then walked to the parsonage, and wrote a check to the church for five hundred dollars and asked the preacher to see that it was applied where it was most needed to further Christ's work. This was not the impulse of a passing moment. This was the consistent practice of a Christian home that had determined the principle of Christian stewardship long ago. This young couple gave as they did because first things had been placed first in their lives.

Some people can be selfish misers operating a peanut stand as readily as some others administering an automobile manufacturing factory. It is not a question of the size of the amount of money involved. It is a question of life's basic governing principles. For a dedicated Christian, it can be nothing less than putting Christ's cause, as represented through his church, first at all times. He knows that he owes it to his church to pay it *up!*

This is my threefold responsibility to my church: I should *pray* it up; I should *say* it up; and I should *pay* it up. And the basic underlying reason is that "Christ loved the church and gave himself up for her, that he might sanctify her, having cleansed her by the washing of water with the word, that the church might be presented before him in splendor, without spot or wrinkle or any such thing, that she might be holy and without blemish" (Eph. 5:25a-27).

7
"INTO ALL THE WORLD"

The early church, in its beginnings, was given its "marching orders" by the risen Christ:

"All authority in heaven and on earth has been given to me. Go therefore and make disciples of all nations, baptizing them in the name of the Father and of the Son and of the Holy Spirit, teaching them to observe all that I have commanded you; and lo, I am with you always, to the close of the age" (Matt. 28:19-20).

The King James Version translates this: "Go ye therefore, and teach all nations." This language seems to place emphasis on the geographical expansion of the church, in an age of discovery, explanation, and settlement in which the human race extended itself around the globe. This kind of translation was appropriate. In fact, in the mid-nineteenth century the study of geography in college and university, which awakened a concern in a group of students' minds to share the benefits of the Christian gospel with newly discovered lands, launched the modern missionary movement.

But today, with all geographical borders crossed and recrossed, and the world shrinking with regard to travel and communication, there seem to be no more lands to conquer. However, it has dawned upon us in more recent years that there are undiscovered and unexplored and "unconquered" areas of human life and experience yet to be taken for Christ and his church. Our Christian objectives have been turned inward instead of outward; to the exploration of human personality and all of its interrelationships, to the great world of the spirit in which too much lies still undiscovered, unexplored, and untaken for our Christ. The newer translation very aptly puts our commission in these words: "Go therefore and make disciples of all nations." The emphasis here is on the person and the person's interrelationships with his fellow men. This is not to be restricted to one nationality, or race, or economic, or social condition, but persons *"out of"* all nations are to be brought into a new relationship through the living Christ in his church.

This is spiritual renewal. It began at Pentecost, but it was essential to the ongoing life of the church. It still is essential. For *renewal* is not a "one shot" experience. Christ's followers are to be renewed day by day. As they respond to his commission to "go into all the world," working together for him, exploring new areas of the spirit and the personality and the social structures, they need his wisdom, his guidance, his enduement. People in the church have not always realized or recognized this, and often there have been periods of weakness and despair and defeat.

We are living in a time when developing interests all

91

around us are making us aware that our basic need is spiritual renewal. We are beginning to recover the understanding that our resources are not in ourselves, but in Jesus Christ. The prophet Isaiah saw this clearly seven centuries before Jesus Chirst came, when he said,

> But they who wait for the Lord
>   shall renew their strength,
> they shall mount up with wings
>   like eagles,
> they shall run and not be weary,
>   they shall walk and not faint (Isa. 40:31).

And before Pentecost could bring his church into existence in the stream of history, Jesus counseled his followers "not to depart from Jerusalem, but to wait for the promise of the Father, which . . . you heard from me" (Acts 1:4).

This is primary and basic, but having "waited" in such a way that the Spirit of the living Christ has taken possession of the church, we must have the willingness to go out into every area of need in the world of human experience to win these worlds for Christ's kingdom.

There are many evidences that this is beginning to happen in many places and in many different ways. Where this happens, spiritual life is quickened, and renewal takes place through the various processes through which the Spirit of God leads. There is today a worldwide interest in such a renewal of the church. The central committee of the World Council of Churches, meeting in Scotland in 1961, made a united confession that this is our deepest need today. It also pointed out that that need must be met and supplied, not only on a general churchwide basis, but especially in local communities where people live and work and play, and where people's lives are intertwined and interrelated. In the Third Assembly of the World Council of Churches that met several months later in New Delhi, this became a major theme and the basis for most of the Assembly's planning. Many denominational gatherings picked up the same accents, under their own dedicated leadership. Pope John XXIII of the Roman Catholic Church called into session the Second Vatican Council for the declared purpose of seeking renewal through Jesus Christ. Pope Paul VI, his successor, followed along these same lines. Everywhere throughout Christendom, a new era of fellowship among Christians was ushered in and grew rapidly. In one outstanding respect, this new movement differed form others that preceded it: There was no effort to arrive at the lowest common denominator in faith and action. Instead, there was open and frank confrontation of differences and their significance, and an honest recognition of the matters of conviction that separate one confession from another, as well as stressing the things that unite men who have faith in Jesus Christ as Saviour and Lord. What will be the scope and character of this new fellowship in Christ, no one has the prophetic ability to foretell. Our prayer is that it will be much more significant and more wonderful than anyone has dreamed.

This calls to mind the witness of history to the first centuries of Christian development and the tremendous influence the church had on the world-community. Tradition tells that the testimony of those who observed and evaluated the church said, "Behold how these Christians love one another." This was the source of their power. They were fulfilling the Lord's prayer of the Upper Room, when he prayed:

I do not pray for these only, but also for those who are to believe in me through their word, that they may all be one; even as thou, Father, art in me, and I in thee, that they also may be in us, so that the world may believe that thou hast sent me. The glory which thou hast given me I have given to them, that they may be one even as we are one, I in them and thou in me, that they may become perfectly one, so that the world may know that thou hast sent me and hast loved them even as thou hast loved me (John 17:20-23).

By way of contrast, when one looks at the attitude toward the church that the world observes today, he sees its brokenness and lack of unity. Frankly, our day is not saying, "Behold, how these Christians love one another."

The historic event that marked the changes of the trend was Constantine's embracing of Christianity. Being greatly impressed at the church's life and fellowship and power for good, this crafty politician decided that this was a good movement to join in order to control and use it. Knowing nothing of the secret of the church's inner power that came from living relationship to Jesus Christ and judging it primarily on the basis of numbers, he proceeded to increase membership in the manner of a political leader. The record says that he marched his armies down to the river's edge and commanded that they be baptized, at the point of spear and sword, whether they wished to be or not. Christians made by the sword—the worst thing that ever happened to the church! As time passed, this action led to such strange manifestations as crusades and religious wars that claimed to further the cause of Jesus Christ, the Prince of Peace, by force of arms and killing. When fighting ceased and peace was established, it was a restless and fearful peace that in 1648 introduced a system of religious controls that uprooted and divided families and made religion within geographical sectors dependent upon the personal and political whims of monarchs and rulers.

In this general period America was colonized, and it was no accident that the most of those who forsook Europe came to America to escape a militarized civilization, blessed by the church. During the nineteenth century there was a growing tension between Christian idealism and a civilization based on power. It was a time of the flowering of the Christian missionary concern for others and, at the same time, the expansion of political empire based on military strength. Inevitably the two became confused in many places, and serious and grave problems developed. There was a "hit-and-miss" sharing of overseas missionary territory that often degenerated into unchristian competition. The impression on non-Christian nationals in various lands caused them to confuse Western culture with Christianity and, like Constantine, to desire the best values of the Christian faith though using the worst non-Christian methods to attain them.

In Tokyo, Japan, during the World Christian Education Convention in 1958, it became evident in a discussion group that the tremendous interest in English Bible classes was not to "get religion," but rather to learn English so the Japanese could read the books that would bring them Western knowledge and power and position. In this country with only 500,000 Christians among eighty-eight million citizens, over five million copies of the English Scriptures had been distributed. This provided textbooks free of charge, classes free of charge, and an open door to Western culture. While many a person was "caught" by the deeper meaning and spirit of Christianity and added to the great influence the small Christian group exerts in the entire population, there were multitudes who experienced nothing of Christian fellowship with Christ or his disciples.

At times, the most promising young people in these overseas lands were brought to America for education and preparation for leadership. Again and again they received terrific shocks to their own faith when they were exposed to a professing Christian culture that made no difference between the non-Christian world and their own profession of faith.

Yet this was not the major experience. The fact is that these were minorities, but they were the evidences of a desperate confusion. In spite of the adulterated expressions of Christian faith and life, "younger churches" grew up and developed in overseas countries, and in recent years became self-conscious and self-contained. In the very nature of the true Christian faith they began to assert themselves as churches. These people began in a very discerning way to reject Western culture, while accepting the way of Jesus Christ. They learned how to make distinction between Standard Oil and Singer Sewing machines and the church of Jesus Christ. These churches have attained their "spiritual majority" and demand that they no longer be treated like colonial territories of Western churches, but as "churches among equals." The result is the rise of the development of Christian fellowship through councils of churches, which are voluntary associations of denominations for cooperation in every area of activity, where they decide they can be more effective witnesses together than they can be separately. The story of the growth of the counciliar movement requires more space than we are able to give it here. This is the means whereby the ecumenical movement has arisen and is endeavoring to rescue the church from the destructive influences that have affected it in recent centuries.

There are those who see grave dangers in the ecumenical movement, simply because they have been misinformed about it and do not understand it. When understood, it is the worldwide expression of the Christian world. The Greek word *oikoumene,* from which our word "ecumenical" derives, means "the whole inhabited world." Applied to the church, it means the whole Christian church in the whole world. Also when understood, it is the inevitable consequence of Christian history, for this is a dedicated effort to seek worldwide unity in Christ—not conformity; not uniformity, but unity. This is the worldwide expression of the Christian movement that becomes one because of its relationship to Jesus Christ.

To the thinking person, this worldwide expression is inevitable and inescapable. This is true, first of all, because the world is shrinking into an intimate neighborhood. This does not mean, of course, that the geographical measurements are changing. Rather, the speed of travel and the transmission of news have so annihilated space that everything becomes public knowledge in our time almost as soon as it happens. Modern transportation and communications have also been the means of "exposing" us, as Christians, before the whole world. We are revealed as a divided Christendom, over against which are the growing powers of the atheistic communistic movement, the renaissance of the ethnic faiths; the growth of materialism, and the victory of hedonism. Over against all these, it is the very nature of Christian faith and action to be one in Christ. This is the logic of a thinking and a believing faith. In it all, there is appearing today a new frankness in facing basic issues together. It is no longer good enough to seek the lowest common denominator, for this leads only to the compounding of weaknesses. So a new spirit of cooperation is slowly emerging. Everywhere there are evidences that there is new interest in vital Christian learning and its meaning.

Overseas, while dissatisfied with our culture and our religion in the midst of our culture, people are nevertheless very interested in Jesus Christ. Here at home there seems to be an increasing interest in understanding God and his universe, and less in the man-made structures and institutions of religion. There is increasing recognition of the worldwide needs of the human family, but inadequate personal response to share in meeting those needs.

In all the world—everywhere—things are being shaken. A worldwide revolution is in progress—in thinking, in planning, in acting. As we face this revolution that is turning the world upside down, there are various attitudes that indicate how people meet it.

Many are afraid because the accustomed things are being shaken. They hanker after the so-called safety and security of "the good old days," and of the "ancient ways," as

Israel confronted by the Red Sea, pursued by the armies of Egypt and taking counsel with their own fears, begin to criticize and find fault with their leaders. How much more comfortable it would be to trust in our ignorance and to be afraid!

Others, forced by the same circumstances, say that this just proves that there is no God, or at least that no one can be certain that there is. Seeing the troubled spirits of others, they seek to take advantage of the confusion and try to throw off all restraint. These are the extremists, who are basically anarchistic by disposition. They cause many others to join those who are afraid, and they, in turn, begin to crusade to defend God, the Bible, Jesus Christ, and the church. They seem to have forgotten that these need no defense. God took care of them long before we came; and he will continue to do so. Robert G. Ingersoll, a brilliant agnostic orator of an earlier generation in this country, predicted about seventy-five years ago in an address in Denver, that within twenty-five years the Bible would be largely forgotten and that copies would be practically unavailable. But Bob Ingersoll is long since dead and almost forgotten by men. On the very spot where he gave this dire prophecy, the American Bible Society has a Bible depot that distributes millions of copies each year. Shades of Ingersoll! "O you, of little faith."

Finally, there are those who know what it means to "trust him and not be afraid." These are the hope of carrying the truth of Jesus Christ into all this world. Emil Brunner, in one of his books, relates the story of his overwhelming experience in climbing a mountain in the Alps in order to welcome the birth of a new day in the resplendent glory of the rising sun reflected in glaciers of multihued majesty and beauty. He climbed all day with a guide, until they came to the cabin where they were to spend the night, so that they could make the last short distance the next morning to welcome the new day. After supper prepared by the guide, they went to sleep in their bunks. The guide had promised that they would awaken in sufficient time to prepare for the final climb and that it would be a most wonderful experience. Dr. Brunner wrote that he had no idea how long he had slept, when suddenly he was awakened by a great roaring noise like cannon going off, or bombs exploding. It seemed to shake the whole mountain. In great fear he jumped out of his bunk and ran to the guide's room to ask whether this were an earthquake. The guide laughed and said, "Go back to sleep. It will be three hours yet before we get up. What you have heard is the sun shining on the other side of the peaks and the glaciers beginning to crack and roar under the heat of the sunshine." So it proved, and when, a few hours later, they climbed to the top and waited for the sun to come across the snow and ice-covered top, it was an experience of ineffable beauty and glory such as he had never had before. To all of this he added that some people are awakened by the sounds of the age in which we live and announce the knell of doom and the end of the world. Others hear the same sounds, and hear the presence of a new and glorious day, just a-borning. As for me, I belong to the latter group when I consider the church of Jesus Christ.

8

MOTIVE IN CHRISTIAN TEACHING

The use of teaching in the life and work of the church is as old as Christianity itself. From the very beginning, the educational method has been closely associated with the church. Its founder and builder was a teacher and was frequently addressed by the title "teacher" in the Gospel records. By means of teaching, he laid the foundations for his church by preparing for leadership a small group who would, in turn, become teachers of others. By all evidences, this was chosen as the prime method for the outreach and growth of the church. Down through the centuries of the Christian era, teaching has never lost its importance. Though neglected at times, it has always been recovered for use as the means of ushering in a new outburst of spiritual power and advance. It seems to be taken for granted in every expression of the church today that teaching is one of its most important functions.

Perhaps we need to ask whether it is taken too much for granted. We who are in the church need to ask ourselves: What is our purpose in Christian teaching? Why teach? If we can find the correct answer to that question, we may be able to bring new life into old forms and methods and stimulate all who are associated with the church to become more effective in the world mission of the Christian church. Of course, the answer depends on our definition of teaching and upon our understanding of the proper relationship of the teaching function of the church to the rest of the activities that are carried on.

What is Christian teaching? Definitions are many and varied. One hardly has time to get acquainted with one when a new and different one is promulgated to take its place. We need to face the fact that agreement on definition here will depend largely upon agreement in theology and in philosophical interpretations of education.

Walter S. Athearn wrote in *The Minister and the Teacher,* that Christian education is "the introduction of controls into experience in terms of Jesus Christ." He went on to explain that

the Christian teacher has but one task, which is to so present Jesus Christ to the rising generation that every act of every day of every person will be performed in harmony with His holy will. There may be such a thing as evangelism that is not educational, but there can be no such thing as a Christian education that is not evangelical. The whole purpose of Christian education is to unite the life of the child with the life of Christ and so lead him to be one with the Father.

If this is accepted, then the teacher must determine his methods and select his materials with this one purpose in view. It is his responsibility to give the child a Christian view of the universe, a Christian view of nature, a Christian view of society, and a Christian view of individual persons. Linked closely with these must be a Christian view of God, of prayer, of property, of all life and its related concerns. The objective is to teach the child to live, move, and have his being in the light of great Christian truths.

"Religious education may be defined as the process of teaching people how to live religiously," writes Georgia Harkness in *Studies in Religious Education*. Dr. Harkness goes on to make her meaning more explicit: "Within recent years there has been more progress in the science and art of teaching religion than in all previous centuries." But she makes it very clear that the progress she refers to is in the development of methods and programs and organization, all of which have expanded the scope of teaching and multiplied the means of teaching. All of these deal with *how* to teach in the church's school. These alone are not enough. Summarizing her further interpretation, I would say that all this is good, for in the past we have paid too little attention to learning *how* to teach religion, with the result that the instruction was often uninteresting and ineffective. Now have come all the improvements in methods, programs, and techniques; yet when one looks at the results, one is inclined to ask whether the children and youth of today are getting a better foundation in biblical knowledge and religious experience than did those of the past. This is not to question the importance of improved methods and materials for teaching in the church, but rather to ask whether religious educators, in their concern to improve pedagogy, have not been inclined to overlook the most important thing in Christian teaching in the church. It is certainly important to know *how* to teach religion, but before anyone can teach the Christian religion effectively, one must have something of his own to teach. Christian teaching involves both form and content, both means and end, both techniques and a philosophy of teaching. If either element is left out of the teaching process, it is incomplete, one-sided, and often dangerous.

In *The Church and Education,* Paul H. Vieth writes these significant words:

Christian education is the process by which persons are confronted with and controlled by the Christian Gospel. It involves the efforts of the Christian community to guide both young and adult persons toward an ever richer possession of the Christian fellowship. It is both individual and social in nature. It is individual because it deals with relating persons to the Christian community and to transforming community life toward an even fuller embodiment of Christian ideals. It is concerned with the past, the present and the future: with the past because it seeks to introduce persons to their religious heritage; with the present because it aims to make religion a vital force in every person's life; with the future because it cultivates creative experiences leading to growth in wisdom and stature and favor with God and man. The foundations of Christian education are to be found in the nature and condition of the man who is to be educated, in the faith which the church professes and in the principles of education which define how learning takes place.[1]

I think this is one of the finest and most complete statements of the purpose and aim of teaching in the Christian

[1] Paul H. Vieth, ed., *The Church and Christian Education* (St. Louis: The Bethany Press, 1947), p. 52. Used by permission.

church that I have ever read. It is worthy of much pondering until its deeper meanings begin to guide us in our teaching programs in the church.

In 1966, the Cooperative Curriculum Project of the Division of Christian Education of the National Council of Churches produced a total curriculum plan, after several years of intensive study and consultation. This was adopted as a guide for the cooperating denominations for developing Christian teaching courses and lesson treatments for their own constituencies. In this authoritative work, *The Church's Educational Ministry,* Christian education is defined as "that ministry of the church which provides the educational undergirding for the church's entire ministry of worship, witness and work. Christian Education is construed as related to all opportunities offered to persons primarily for the purpose of education in the Christian faith and for Christian mission."

In setting forth the purpose of Christian education this work states,

The objective for Christian education is that all persons be aware of God through his self-disclosure, especially his redeeming love as revealed in Jesus Christ and that they respond in faith and love—to the end that they may know who they are and what their human situation means, grow as sons of God rooted in the Christian community, live in the Spirit of God in every relationship, fulfill their common discipleship in the world and abide in Christian hope.

Summarizing these foregoing definitions in a succinct and yet comprehensive statement, I believe that it is the purpose of Christian education to lead persons into a vital experience of faith in Jesus Christ as Savior and Lord and into living membership in his church. As living units in the church body, they are prepared for and guided into Christian living and service in all of life's interrelationships. Christian instruction endeavors to help persons achieve the abundant life in well-rounded Christian character and to Christianize all of life's relationships.

These definitions and interpretations are a relatively modern development in the field of Christian education, but their basic concepts are as old as Christianity itself. It is a characteristic trait of man to seek to extend his most cherished beliefs and experiences to others. He teaches them to his children, he seeks to persuade and convert his fellow men. Even if he did not consciously teach his beliefs, he would still pass them on to those who are most closely associated with him by the influence which comes through living together.

The church has always shown zeal for nurturing her children in the faith as well as for winning adult converts. This educational zeal was cradled in the Hebrew synagogue school. Its origin is the directive from Moses, given in Deut. 6:4-9, which every Hebrew child has to memorize and understand:

Hear O Israel: The Lord our God is one Lord; and you shall love the Lord your God with all your heart, and with all your soul, and with all your might. And these words which I command you this day shall be upon your heart; and you shall teach them diligently to your children, and shall talk of them when you sit in your house, and when you walk by the way, and when you lie down, and when you rise. And you shall bind them as a sign upon your hand, and they shall be as frontlets between your eyes. And you shall write them on the doorposts of your house and on your gates.

G. Walter Fiske writes in *Studies in Religious Education* that

In the spirit of this great passage the Boy of Nazareth was undoubtedly taught religion in his childhood. Later, he became the Master-Teacher, demonstrating in his remarkable technique that a church may live by teaching. St. Paul seemed to be another born teacher, and he and the teachers he taught carried the Christian faith into its third and fourth generation. In the Gentile world, it was their difficult task to transform pagans into Christians. They were too wise to think this could be done suddenly, in a single session. It could not be accomplished by a single inspirational experience. It required a long educational and nurturing process. So they set up their schools for inquirers who wished to know what it really meant to be a Christian; and these inquirers were faithfully taught for two or three years before they were received as full members of the church.

Dr. Fiske goes on in his study to state that after Christianity became popular as the established religion of the Roman Empire, religious teaching for the masses waned. For the next one thousand years its aim was chiefly ecclesiastical, being concerned with the training of priests and monks for the future leadership of the church.

The Protestant Reformation brought a revival of the importance of Christian teaching and on a broadly democratic basis. At first, the purpose was largely doctrinal. It was to teach the new creeds of the churches of the Reformation. After some time, this gradually gave way to the "knowledge of the Bible" aim, as printed Bibles became more numerous near the close of the eighteenth century. About this time, Sunday schools were organized in England and in America. Soon the evangelistic aim was added to the biblical aim, and during the nineteenth century these continued as the chief objectives of the church's teaching. In the first part of the twentieth century, with the development of modern child study, psychology and education theories and principles, Christian education developed several new aims in various directions —the pupil-centered aim; the social or Christian citizenship aim; the Christian character aim; and the creative experience aim—depending on the leader's special training and emphasis or on the denomination's theological position. Often there has resulted a one-sidedness when these various aims have been stressed one at a time, or when there was no adequate overall Christian education philosophy to keep the purpose definitely centered in the purposes of Jesus Christ. This created a period of confusion in which Christian education was often misrepresented and opposed because of the one-sided approach of its own proponents. In too many churches this resulted in creating a suspicion that religious education was not Christian and was the enemy of evangelism and the other functions of a total church program. It frequently came about that the curricula and methods in local church schools were not in harmony with the basic concepts of the Christian religion.

Three general trends during this period tended to create this condition. First was the so-called scientific method which tried to apply materialistic, scientific tests to metaphysical and ethical principles and ideals, which led to a narrowness and superficiality in both curriculum content and instruction methods, because of the lack of a sound Christian philosophy of education. However, this must not be used to decry the scientific and pragmatic method, but is stated here as a warning that the persons who use this method should be individuals of such ethical and moral character that they will use it truthfully. The second trend is the tendency to borrow from public education without considering carefully that the teaching of spiritual truth is in a different field of experience than mathematics, physics, chemistry, biology, or similar fields of science. Too much current public educational theory is still based on humanistic behavioral psychology and pragmatic philosophy. The third tendency is to substitute techniques for content. This came about largely through following the progressive theories of education in which methods, organization, plans, and programs to produce artificial life-situations to stimulate the repetition of certain reactions in order to habituate them and thus produce character traits are the chief concerns. In this connection, I admit that organization and methodology are important and valuable, but any education that is basically Christian must hold these as secondary requirements, not primary requirements.

Back in the early 1930's, when Harold McAfee Robinson was chairman of the International Council of Religious Education, he declared in opening an annual session: "We have been paying a lot of attention to methods, techniques, programs, and procedures in our work of Christian education, and rightly so, but it is time now that we pay more attention to what happens to persons when they are taught the truth that is in Christ." That statement marked a definite turning point in the basic emphases in the International Council of Christian Education and in the co-operative work that it sponsored. A new emphasis on persons emerged and gave what some called "evangelistic motivation" to the work of Christian teaching.

We began to see once more that the world cannot be saved by pedagogy alone. There must be teaching, of course, by means of all of the best tested methods and techniques. But we need to know that there is also a subject-matter, a content, of the Christian religion, and for our purpose in Christian education, that content is the Christian gospel. The teacher of our religious faith must have a clear conception of the relation of Christian truth to all relationships and experiences in life. This teacher must endeavor to make the great basic Christian concepts the possession of all the people. Regrettably, the average Sunday school teacher, in recent years, does not have this information. As a result, religious fanaticisms and vagaries spread rapidly in these times. There are certain essentials of Christian truths which are necessary to the development of the Christian religion among the people, and these essential truths must become powerful elements of faith to be lived out in daily experiences in every contact in which man lives. Pedagogy, or teaching, is an instrument to this end, but pedagogy must not become a substitute for Christian content. Every effective system of education must bring the rising generation into possession of the selected and socially serviceable cultures and experiences of humankind. This must not be condemned as "indoctrination" or stigmatized as "transmission" and the technique or method then glorified at the expense of content. There *is* a gospel message without which there can be no Christian education.

This understanding of the aim and content in Christian education leads to the fundamental conclusion that Christian teaching is the responsibility of the whole church and not of some segment or sub-organization of it. The church alone is competent to carry so great a responsibility and to underake so great a task. Luther A. Weigle, formerly Dean of Yale Divinity School, has stated it this way: "In a general but vital and fundamental sense the whole life of the Christian church is an educational enterprise, and its entire work is that of teaching." Harry Munro, at one time on the staff of the International Council of Religious Education, has written an excellent book on this thesis: *The Church As a School.* It was read far and wide and did much to make this working-principle known throughout America.

Of course, such statements can easily be misinterpreted and made to mean that organizationally, the agencies of Christian education are the church. This is not true and never should be so interpreted. The organized Christian education agencies are the tools (the servants) of the church, which the church has created and which the church must use in the ways that will best serve to achieve the supreme purpose of the church itself. The point of view here is that the church itself is the only adequate agency for Christian teaching. It may express itself through the utilization of the several agencies that have been developed, such as the Sunday school, the young people's society, vacation church school, and training classes, but it is only as these are integrated into the total life of the church that Christian education can become truly effective. Dr. Vieth writes that

the teaching program of the church requires that some of the more mature members share their fuller understanding of, and commitment to, the Christian faith, with those who are less mature. This calls for classes, discussion groups and opportunities to practice Christian living. It makes use of books, lesson materials, pictures, maps and equipment of all sorts. It employs classrooms, time schedules and organizational arrangements. All these teaching activities, taken together, constitute the church school. Such a school may include any and all of the agencies that have been developed for this purpose and other activities that do not fit into any of these agencies. These teaching-learning activities are for young and old, for all must undergo the discipline which will yield growth in knowledge, understanding, attitudes and skill in living the Christian life.[2]

All of this leads to the conclusion that in the church's Christian teaching, the sense of content and aim is the concern of the whole church—that the teaching work of the church as our organized method or means must be the servant of all. To try to make this much more clear, let me point out that there are a number of basic functional expressions of the Christian life which have their counterparts in the Christian church's teaching and serving program. These are worship, evangelism, missions, stewardship, and Christian social action. These are in addition

[2] *The Church and Christian Education,* p. 95.

to Christian education. When each of these is simply defined, it becomes relatively easy to see their interrelatedness and interdependence. They are really not separate and distinct functions, but various expressions of the Christian faith and life in personal experience and in the life and work of the church. Any one of these, standing alone, is fractional or fragmentary. All of these together constitute a full-rounded, well-balanced, and unified expression of the Christian life in action. The church should certainly be concerned with all of these areas, not just with one or two to the exclusion of the others. Those whom the church has called to guide and direct others in the whole life of faith and action ought surely to be interested and concerned with this total educational mission also.

More specifically, worship is primarily an attitude toward God and a spiritual outreach after him, both personal and corporate—a seeking and a finding of fellowship with him. Evangelism is a spirit, a passion, a climate, a dynamic that seeks to relate persons to God through faith in Jesus Christ as Savior and Lord. It should not be restricted to any one method but should endue and empower all good and legitimate methods whereby the good news in Jesus Christ may be shared. Missions is the field of operations beyond the local or parish community, in which this evangelistic spirit seeks expression in winning others to Christian discipleship. Stewardship is the acknowledgement of God's ownership and rulership in all of life and the acceptance of our responsibility as Christians to devote life, talent, time, and means to Christ's work and purposes. Christian social action is the manifestation

113

in human society through Christian disciples, of the way the Christian faith expresses itself in all relationships in life. Christian education is a method, a system of plans and procedures and teaching courses, a set of skills and techniques. In short, it is a set of tools and blueprints for implementing these other functions of the Christian church.

Strictly speaking, Christian education has no content of its own. There is a content in worship, a content in evangelism; a content in stewardship; a content in missions; a content in Christian social action. All of these have their ultimate source in the Bible, the revelation of God's truth, and in Christian experience. But Christian education must employ the content of all these others to formulate and develop the teaching materials that should be shared with other disciples in all expressions of life to bring them to commitment to Jesus Christ as Savior and lead them into loyalty to him as Lord. Therefore, the content of the curriculum of Christian education is completely dependent upon the other functions of the church program. Christian education can have no purpose or existence apart from them. Instead, it should be the servant of all.

Christian Education should teach, but with a purpose that is basically evangelistic in its deepest, highest, and widest sense. Its aim is to bring persons to Christ by saving faith and then to bring them to maturity in him through nurture and service in a growing Christian life. This it should do in the church at home, just as it seeks to do in the church in the mission field, for fundamentally, there is no difference. This it should do through dedicated persons who willingly accept their stewardship responsibilities under God. Furthermore, in all the relationships in human society, it should show how Christian action is the solution for all of society's ills. Therefore, the program of Christian education that would serve the kingdom of God in the largest and best possible way must take all of these functions into consideration, utilize their content in a comprehensive program of action, and through such a program, seek to bring persons to commit themselves to Jesus Christ as Savior and Lord, thereby entering into his fellowship and way of living.

The apostle Paul made this clear to the Ephesian churches when he wrote them in his church epistle:

But grace was given to each of us according to the measure of Christ's gift. Therefore it is said,

"When he ascended on high he led a host of captives and he gave gifts to men."

. . . And his gifts were that some should be apostles, some prophets, some evangelists, some pastors and teachers, for the equipment of the saints, for the work of ministry [Christian service], for building up the body of Christ [the church], until we all attain to the unity of the faith and of the knowledge of the Son of God, to mature manhood, to the measure of the stature of the fullness of Christ; so that we may no longer be children, tossed to and fro and carried about with every wind of doctrine, by the cunning of men, by their craftiness in deceitful wiles. Rather, speaking the truth in love, we are to grow up in every way into him who is the head, into Christ, from whom the whole body, joined and knit together by every joint with which it is supplied, when each part is working properly, makes bodily growth and upbuilds itself in love (Eph. 4:7-16).

In the Bible, there is the record of two different water basins. In the case of the first one, a Roman governor took a basin of water and, before a crowd of people who high-pressured him, endeavored to wash his hands of all responsibility for the injustice the crowd was insisting upon. His purpose was to protect the organization—in this case political—and to maintain the status quo for selfish reasons. Pilate's story stands today as the record of base cowardice and servile fear. In the other case, a humble peasant teacher took a basin of water and, in a group of intimate friends, stooped to wash the stains of daily toil and travel off their feet—the lowliest and most menial of slave services. He did not seek to escape responsibility, nor did he seek to save an organization to perpetuate selfish desire for power over others. Instead, he demonstrated in the midst of his awed followers what he had taught them by word of mouth: "Whoever would be great among you must be your servant." This action of Jesus stands as a challenge to all his followers to this very day. This is also the challenge to Christian education. In fact, this is the only place that Christian teaching can occupy in the church of Christ—not lording it over other functions of the church, but gladly and freely offering its ministry to strengthen all the work and to cooperate with all others in the building up of the church. To this purpose, Christian teaching was committed by the great teacher when the church was launched. In our day, we should follow in his steps.

9

OUR SPIRITUAL HERITAGE

There are many people in our churches today who have a tremendous interest in the renewal of the church. But, I want to call attention to the fact that many of those who are speaking of renewal do not seem to be aware of our heritage from the past. Until we have some understanding and appreciation of this heritage, we cannot understand what renewal is and whom it involves. Therefore, we must turn our attention to our debt to the past. All that has gone before in the Christian movement is foundational to the present and is important and influential for the future. On the capital frieze of the National Archives Building in Washington, D.C., chiseled in large letters is this legend: "All History Is Prologue." Everything that has gone ahead has been preparation for today. But it is also true that "tomorrow is here." The prophesy of what will be can already be discerned in what has come to pass. So it is with the church. Jesus Christ has not only built his church, but it is just as important to understand that Jesus Christ is building his church now—preparing it for its ultimate glorification.

It is important then that we know something about our spiritual heritage in the church of Christ. When we speak of heritage, we usually think in terms of family relationships: one generation passing on its experiences and ideals to the next generation, and so on. Each generation blesses, or condemns, the succeeding generation with the heritage it passes along. It is even so with the generations of the people of God who are members of the church. The Christian home has a place of tremendous importance in the life and work of the church for today and for tomorrow.

The apostle Paul, writing to his spiritual son Timothy, stated it like this:

To Timothy, my beloved child: . . . I thank God whom I serve with a clear conscience, as did my fathers, when I remember you constantly in my prayers. As I remember your tears, I long night and day to see you, that I may be filled with joy. I am reminded of your sincere faith, a faith that dwelt first in your grandmother Lois and your mother Eunice and now, I am sure, dwells in you. Hence I remind you to rekindle the gift of God that is within you through the laying on of my hands; for God did not give us a spirit of timidity but a spirit of power and love and self-control. Do not be ashamed then of testifying to our Lord, nor of me his prisoner, but take your share of suffering for the gospel in the power of God (II Tim. 1:1-1-8).

In this passage I call attention to these words: "I am reminded of your sincere faith, a faith that dwelt first in your grandmother Lois and your mother Eunice and now, I am sure, dwells in you." Your grandmother Lois and your mother Eunice, and you. Three generations!

Here we see the importance of Christian fathers and mothers and Christian grandfathers and grandmothers passing along the Christian heritage to their children and their children's children. Someone has written that "Christianity is always just one generation removed from extinction." This is another way of saying that if the Christian faith and life die out in us and are not shared with our children, they become extinct so far as our own families are concerned. For this heritage cannot be passed along in the bloodstream. It has nothing to do with genetics, the transmission of physical characteristics or intellectual traits. This is, instead, a matter of the impact of the quality and character of the religious life, or spiritual being, of the parents exerted upon children in the fellowship of the family and the home.

This is no new discovery, but rather a recovery of a very significant tried and tested truth. I could illustrate this from numerous examples in Christian history, but I want to relate a much more modern application of it. Since 1953, it has been my privilege to make regular visits to Germany to supervise the congregations and conferences of my own denomination. I have been able to get into East Berlin and to confer with leaders and members of our denomination behind the Iron Curtain in East Germany. By means of firsthand witnessing, I learned much about Christian faithfulness under persecution and suffering. Frequently I have called on Bishop Otto Dibelius, of the Landeskirche of Berlin-Brandenburg, to discuss the situation among his people in East Germany and to compare notes. On one of the last visits, he told me that his leaders were noting a new interest in worship services, including an increase in attendance, on the part of young people. After forty years of the atheistic government's effort to kill religion and faith in God by means of atheistic teaching in the school system, the Christian faith is on the increase among youth as never before in this generation. This verified what I had learned from my own churchmen. I wanted to get at the *reason* for this change, so I questioned Bishop Dibelius about it. His answer was very revealing: "You know, when God created mothers, he gave them an inordinate love for their children. The communist powers forgot to take this into account. By the silent life-giving power of mother love, children were growing up and returning to church and to vital Christian faith." He went on to point out that the parents, especially the mothers, had a deep, abiding faith in God. When their babies came, they cradled them in their arms with love, sang Christian hymns to croon them to sleep, and prayed aloud for them by name. The infant breathed in the Christian atmosphere of such a home. In these first years, when the child could not reason or understand, even before he could speak, he was surrounded with all the evidences of Christian love.

My wife's mother, who was a good, pious member of the Swiss Reformed Church, reared ten children by this formula, teaching them to fold their hands and bow their heads at prayer time, long before they could understand why. This left a deposit of awe and worship as a precious heritage to each one of them.

This is what Bishop Dibelius pointed out to me in

Berlin, but he went on to state that when school age came, these children were exposed to the efforts of atheistic teachers trying to destroy their faith by idolizing science, worshiping the state, and trying to kill God. Then came the questioning adolescent years when youth wants to know the reason why; this is because God makes man to grow this way. They want now to know whether mother and grandmother, father and grandfather are right about the Christian faith or whether the teachers are right in saying there is nothing to faith in God. Many of them search for information, facts, and the experiences of others. To learn more about religion, they have to go to the worship services of the church. There is no other place where this is being taught. Sunday schools, youth societies, scout troops are all forbidden by law. No classes in religion can be conducted. The only place where they can hear these truths interpreted is in the church worship service. This is why Bishop Dibelius issued advice to his pastors to become teachers in the pulpit while they preached, in order to give these young people the message they so much need. This is why increasing numbers of them are becoming active in the churches because the spiritual heritage from their parents and grandparents is becoming alive in their own experiences. So the "faith that dwelt first in your grandmother Lois and your mother Eunice" is manifesting itself in the present generation as it enters into its spiritual heritage.

This means of blessing our children and our children's children is as old as the Hebrew educational method in religious teaching. In his farewell addresses, Moses gave the children of Israel this plan, and it is operative among

Hebrews to the present day. In Deut. 6:4-7, we read: "Hear, O Israel: The Lord our God is one Lord; and you shall love the Lord your God with all your heart, and with all your soul, and with all your might. And these words which I command you this day shall be upon your heart; and you shall teach them diligently to your children." Moses continued to explain the family and home situations in which this teaching-sharing process was carried on.

I remind you that Lois and Eunice were Hebrew mothers who belonged to the people who followed this plan. They followed the same principles of religious nurture that Salome followed in rearing James and John; that Mary followed in bringing up Jesus in Nazareth; that the mother of Paul followed in Tarsus; that Elizabeth followed in nurturing John the Baptist. They each prepared their sons for the time of voluntary entrance into the status of "sons of the law" and into manhood's full ecclesiastical estate. With Jesus, this was at the age of twelve when he was taken to Jerusalem to undergo the examination at the hands of the doctors of the law and to be initiated by approved rites into the religious fellowship. In the case of Timothy, Paul reminds him of this and exhorts him to "rekindle the gift of God that is within you."

What an example these Hebrew mothers set for us Christians—especially those of us who claim to be of Christ's church in our time! We get so engrossed in the gadgets and conveniences of our inventive and affluent age that we lose all sense of obligation for the religious nurture of our own children. We delegate this responsibility to the church school or to the public school, with a kind of blind faith that seems to believe that an irregular half hour on Sunday morning and five minutes in the opening of the school day will suffice to give our children a Christian heritage upon which they can build their spiritual lives. This is impossible! The average attendance of most children in Sunday school is fifty percent of the Sundays in a year, which totals just thirteen hours of such instruction in an entire year. And who will claim that all thirteen hours are equally good and valuable for the child?

When the United States Supreme Court rendered the decision that prohibits schools from conducting official worship periods in the schools under school authority, because of our principle of the separation of church and state, many of our citizens were aroused in furor against the Court and all who agreed with it. Most of these people were never concerned enough, or fair enough in their arguments, to read first the actual decision and understand what it does or does not say. But after the decision was widely read and studied, all of the major denominations in their plenary meetings one by one supported the Supreme Court decision. They were keenly aware of the fact that our Christian heritage cannot be transmitted to our children by a few minutes of religious "exercises" at the beginning of the school day. They became more concerned that our homes and churches overcome their apathy and irresponsibility and accept their Christian obligations to give their children the opportunity to choose the Christian way, even as their ancestors did before them. The Supreme Court decision has stabbed many of us awake to our negligence and our duty!

In the wake of this decision, new educational movements are being developed to teach the Bible for credit in the schools and colleges, as good literature and history, with all of the moral and ethical values that it exhibits in its many books. No one can be truly educated who has not read and studied these masterpieces of the past. Increasing numbers of our educational institutions are introducing such classes. This is very important to counteract our present-day religious illiteracy.

But this can never substitute for real religion nor satisfy our children's spiritual hungers, which are the essential parts of our spiritual heritage. The basic responsibility still rests on "your grandmother Lois and your mother Eunice." I have already called attention to the fact that these were Hebrew mothers. Christianity, as such, had not yet been launched as a church of the living Christ. They did what was good and necessary in their day, but it was not until Paul guided Timothy into the full flowering of faith in Jesus Christ that the heritage was quickened and made alive in his experience. These mothers gave Timothy the best religious culture possible up to their time, but such culture, important as it is, is not enough.

Our Christian heritage goes beyond Christian culture, for a very important part of that heritage is faith in Christ, alive in the life and work of the individual and the family. That is why Paul wrote: "Hence I remind you to rekindle the gift of God that is within you through the laying on of my hands; for God did not give us a spirit of timidity but a spirit of power and love and self-control." The New English Bible puts this in even more striking language:

That is why I now remind you to stir into flame the gift of God which is within you through the laying on of my hands. For the spirit that God gave us is no craven spirit, but one to inspire strength, love, and self-discipline. So never be ashamed of your testimony to our Lord, nor of me his prisoner, but take your share of suffering for the sake of the Gospel, in the strength that comes from God.

We need to guard against the error of mistaking the Christian culture in our heritage for the acceptance of Christ as Savior and the commitment to him as Lord, involved in faith. "Stir into flame the gift of God which is within you." This is a "plus" element that is the spiritual earmark of vital Christianity. It has been an important element that is necessary in every worthwhile reformation or renewal movement in the church. Martin Luther set it over against the forms and hierarchical methods in the Roman Catholic Church and lighted reformation fires both inside and outside the church. John Wesley and his co-workers stirred up the Church of England in their time with their emphasis on spiritual reality, namely, the life-changing experience of surrender to the Holy Spirit. This Anglican priest was befriended by a group of Moravians on a sailing vessel that took him as a missionary to the colony of Georgia. He was impressed by their simple piety and later on, in London, attended one of their prayer meetings in a little worship place on Aldersgate Street, where, he said, he was "strangely" moved, and his heart was warmed as he opened up his life to the control of the Holy Spirit. I have sometimes wondered how much of this spiritual endowment could be traced back to the godly influence of John Wesley's mother, Susanna. Here came to full flower her spiritual concern for her children, and there were seventeen. This spiritual "plus" is the heritage of The Methodist Church and other churches, from John Wesley.

Philip William Otterbein was born in a German Reformed parsonage at Dillenberg in West Germany, and under this parsonage influence he came to respond to the call to missionary service in the new North American colonies of England. He came to minister to German-speaking settlers and was confronted by the formalities and the cold veneer of European state church practices of that time. Breaking out of this shell, he associated himself with groups in the new spiritual movement that history calls "the Great Awakening." Cutting through denominational lines, he united in worship and service with all who believed in the personal and spiritual work of the Holy Spirit, operative in the lives of people. He was the center of the United Brethren movement.

Jacob Albright, a moral religionist of the strictest sort, prided himself on his rectitude and his performance of religious duties on Sunday, but when tragedy struck his family in the sudden death of three children in an epidemic, he did not know where to turn. It takes more than formal creeds and pious practices to meet such upheavals. He was driven to days of prayer and wrote in his daily journal: "I was converted deep into eternal life." He began to pray for pastoral care for his German-speaking neighbors until his own mind and heart were led to face the call, and then he began to dedicate his life to a tireless preaching career that resulted in the beginning of the

Evangelical Association, later called The Evangelical Church.

In each of these cases, the religious culture served as a necessary matrix but, the spiritual gift had to be stirred into flame. This soon kindled the hearts of others, and the fires spread.

However, the kindling of the flame within is not just for starting conflagrations that will spread irresponsibly. There must be no ignoring the heritage—the whole Christian culture that is the bearer of our spiritual heritage. I believe in a Christian education that nurtures growing life and shares the whole Christian heritage but that does not stop at exposure to culture. Instead, it seeks to bring the person into vital encounter and relationship with Jesus Christ. It should not be burdened with methods of creedal indoctrination, the recital of theological formularies, and mass baptisms, with no stirring into flame the gift of God. To kindle this spiritual flame is not easy. That is why Paul wrote: "The spirit that God gave us is no craven spirit, but one to inspire strength, love, and self-discipline. So never be ashamed of your testimony to our Lord, nor of me his prisoner, but take your share of suffering for the sake of the Gospel, in the strength that comes from God" (NEB).

Here is a call to spiritual boldness. It speaks of courage, love, and order; it emphasizes testimony, growth, and discipline. These are the chief elements of our inheritance in the church of Christ, which have been shared with us by our forebears and on which we can build and grow for tomorrow. This involves a living, daily witness to the presence of Jesus Christ in our manner of life. It engenders a desire to improve, to grow, to become more Christ-like, with its exhortation to become "perfect" as he is "perfect." It also ought to include a group discipline that will save the individual from tangential spiritual vagaries.

Dr. E. Stanley Jones has pointed out that the well-ordered Christian life involves *three* basic principles. First, one must get acquainted with the Jesus of history, and this requires knowledge of the Gospel records and the surrounding writings of the Old and New Testaments. Second, one must meet the Christ of experience in personal and living encounter on the basis of our knowledge gained from the records. And third, there must be the commitment of our experience and testimony to the discipline of the group of fellow Christians to which we belong, lest our individual judgments lead us astray from the truth that the church finds in Christ.

This is not a program for timid people, or for those of a craven spirit, or cowards. This calls for courage of the highest order. I have been thrilled at what I have learned about such courage in East Germany and in Hong Kong and what I have heard from Czechoslovakia, Hungary, Poland, Russia, and East Germany. Many have learned at first hand what it can cost to be vital Christians, with more than an outward form of godliness.

Then why are so many of us in affluent and favored America fearful in this regard? Why is there not more active concern about giving our children and grandchildren a fair chance at a Christian heritage? The purpose is not to try to produce little duplicates of the past but to "stir into flame the gift of God" in order for them to serve this present age as their grandparents served theirs. We need to raise up courageous witnesses who will dare to meet the issues of this day as the prophets and apostles and other Christians in their time met theirs. We need men and women who, like the men and women in our spiritual heritage, will commit everything to the Lord Christ for the sake of the world for which he died and rose again.

I was a thirteen-year-old high school lad that winter when I took my public stand for Jesus Christ. It was in a church in Minnesota where my father was the pastor. He had spoken to me privately of his fatherly concern for my spiritual commitment and growth. However, this was not the first time I had given thought to my relationship to God. I was the son of a parsonage, a regular Sunday school and church attendant (under parental duress at times, to be sure), and I was regularly exposed to Christian culture in every normal way. Father and mother fostered and expressed family religion, and it was not unusual for us children to hear our names mentioned in petitions at family prayers. But there came the night when, of my own volition, I wanted to declare myself for Christ and to commit myself to the Christian way. According to the customs in that church, I went forward to the church altar and knelt in prayer as a public token of my commitment. Suddenly a man knelt beside me, put his arm around my shoulders, and said, "Reuben, just thank Jesus Christ for what he has done to bring you forgiveness of sin and ask him to lead you into a new life of fellowship with him. You don't have to beg him, or plead with him. Just simply and quietly thank him for it all and believe it." This was the pastor, but he was my father, too. He helped me to pray the prayer of simple faith and to begin my great adventure of following Jesus Christ. Little did I know, or even realize, what my father must have experienced that night as he helped his son to pray and believe.

Years later, when I was pastor in a church in South Bend, Indiana, I frequently extended invitations to any who desired to confess Christ as Savior and Lord before the congregation to come forward to the altar as a sign of such commitment. One Sunday night I had barely started such an invitation when a little nine-year-old girl left her mother's side in a pew near the back and walked all alone down a long center aisle to the place of prayer. As she knelt to pray, I was at her side, knelt with her, slipped my arm around her, and said, "Margaret, thank him for calling you, and simply and quietly say to him that you will follow him from tonight on." As our daughter made her commitment that night to Jesus Christ as Savior and Lord, I, her father, knew what a great joy a parent can experience as he has a personal part in guiding his child into this spiritual heritage of faith.

10
THE NEW CHURCH

All over Christendom there is talk of the need for renewal of the church. It is said that what we need is a *new* church. The church that needs renewal is the human manifestation of *his* church. The men and women who are being built into his church are still in need of growth and development as they move on to maturity in Christ. From this point of view, the church does need renewal.

The "newest" church I know of is the church of Pentecost; the church of the Upper Room. It is true that it was born in the first century A.D., but the record of it in the book of Acts sounds like the newest thing in churches, just reported in the public press:

While the Day of Pentecost was running its course they were all together in one place, when suddenly there came from the sky a noise like that of a strong driving wind, which filled the whole house where they were sitting. And there appeared to them tongues like flames of fire, dispersed among them and resting on each one. And they were all filled with the Holy Spirit and began to talk in other tongues, as the Spirit gave them power of utterance.

Now there were living in Jerusalem devout Jews drawn from every nation under heaven; and at this sound the crowd gathered, all bewildered because each one heard the apostles talking in his own language. They were amazed and in their astonishment exclaimed, 'Why, they are all Galileans, are they not, these men who are speaking? How is it then that we hear them, each of us in his own native language? Parthians, Medes, Elamites; inhabitants of Mesopotamia, of Judaea and Cappadocia, of Pontus and Asia, of Phrygia and Pamphylia, of Egypt and the districts of Libya around Cyrene; visitors from Rome, both Jews and proselytes, Cretans and Arabs, we hear them telling in our own tongues the great things God has done.' And they were all amazed and perplexed, saying to one another, 'What can this mean?' Others said contemptuously, 'They have been drinking.'

But Peter stood up with the Eleven, raised his voice, and addressed them: 'Fellow Jews, and all you who live in Jerusalem, mark this and give me a hearing. These men are not drunk, as you imagine; for it is only nine in the morning. No, this is what the prophet spoke of: "God says, 'This will happen in the last days; I will pour out upon everyone a portion of my spirit; and your sons and daughters shall prophesy; your young men shall see visions, and your old men shall dream dreams. Yes, I will endue even my slaves, both men and women, with a portion of my spirit, and they shall prophesy. And I will show portents in the sky above, and signs on the earth below—blood and fire and drifting smoke. The sun shall be turned to darkness, and the moon to blood, before that great, resplendent day, the day of the Lord, shall come. And then, everyone who invokes the name of the Lord shall be saved'" (Acts 2:1-21 NEB).

After reading that, I ask myself whether the church, as we manifest it today, is like that church described in those words, and I am compelled to answer, "No, not very much like it. We suffer by comparison!" But, I must hasten to add, "However, I see a change coming. There is growing concern for the church among us, a deep movement of the Holy Spirit underway in the church of our time. It is like "the sound of marching in the tops of the balsam trees." (I Chr. 14:15 RSV.) We see it as a cloud on the horizon, the size of a man's hand, but it is prophetic of spiritual outpourings to come. I believe that we are on the threshold of a new advance for the church of Jesus Christ, a new way that points to a "new" church. But it is still the same church that was born on Pentecost Day almost two thousand years ago. Since that beginning, there have been times of decay and weakness because of our humanity, followed by times of resurgence, new outpouring, and spiritual power. There have been times of reformation and revival, in which things were made new. It is such a new church that I have in mind. And it is such renewal that I believe will soon be manifested in its life and work.

I am well aware of the fact that there are many who will not agree with me. In fact, there are two general classes of people in our churches who would take different points of view. First, there are those who are positive in their belief that the "church dispensation" is about to come to an end; that the knell of doom is being sounded, and that hell will break forth on the earth soon as a prelude to judgment. Then will come a millenium of peace according to them. These are the religionists of today who sit in judgment upon all others who do not agree with, or accept, their apocalyptic predictions. They are absolutely certain

133

that those who disagree with them are wrong and are spiritually lost. What is amazing is that they seem to be unified among themselves in their attacks upon such things as councils of churches, the Revised Standard Version of the Bible, denominational seminaries, and cooperative missionary programs; but in matters such as the mode of baptism, speaking in tongues, dispensationalism, and denominational structure, they are as far apart among themselves as they are from more liberal Christianity.

Several years ago one of these religious dissenters withdrew from the denomination in which he had been ordained, because he followed the leadership of a brilliant seminary professor under whom he had studied and whom he followed in opposition to his denominational leadership. This withdrawal happened almost simultaneously with his "unfrocking" by his church. Taking a small contingent of followers with them, the two formed a "true" church; but hardly a year had passed when these two leaders were at odds, and they split their little group into two denominations. It happens again and again. United by their common opposition to the historic churches, the dissenters cannot agree among themselves. This kind of person has no faith in a new manifestation of spiritual renewal in the church of our time, except by apocalyptic catastrophe, and even this has to be according to his private interpretation. I do not say that Christ cannot reveal himself in such an apocalyptic fashion; I only say that I do not know how or when our Lord Jesus Christ will manifest himself anew in his church. He said that it was our part to be occupied in the life and work of his church, whenever he comes in a new manifestation, or in whatever way he comes.

The other group that has no apparent faith in the renewal of the church—the revelation of the *new* church—is at the other extreme of the theological pole. Those who belong here are usually called ultraliberals. They are certain that the day of the Christian church is past. They write learned articles about the "post-Christian" and the "post-Protestant" period into which history has entered. They teach that the influence of the church and of the Christian standards it teaches and preaches, are noneffective as far as the real important movements of our times are concerned. In our present pluralistic society, they claim that a Protestant moral ethic is no longer effective; the Christian leader doesn't count, and for some of them, "God is dead." It is a dark and dreary spiritual picture that they draw.

I do not suppose that one man's experience in this regard can be considered a successful refutation of such arguments, but I have not found their arguments convincing. When one thinks of the claims of those who prophesy the end of the Christian era, the statement of G. K. Chesterton, the English essayist, comes to mind. It was made about Christianity, but it applies equally well to the church. Wrote Mr. Chesterton: "The Christian ideal has not been tried and found wanting; it has been found difficult and left untried." And even so, I say that this talk about a post-Christian age compels me to state that we have never really had a truly Christian church age yet. This is still the future goal toward which we move. Our goal is the *new church* that is in process of *becoming*. This is the church that Jesus Christ is building—the church for which he gave his life upon the cross, and took it again in the resurrection, and set his church in the world as his witness by the power of that resurrection.

Those of us who believe in this church stand in between these two extremes that I have described. But standing here, I believe that we stand with Jesus Christ and his church. This I claim, in spite of the general circumstances of our times, in personal, social, political, and international affairs. Looking at it merely from the human point of view, one could view the present scene and fervently recite Hamlet's plaint: "The time is out of joint; O cursed spite that ever I was born. . . ." But the times are always "out of joint." It was so in Hammurabi's time, eighteen hundred years before Christ, as evidenced by inscriptions on the baked clay tiles that could be literal descriptions of conditions in our day. They were "out of joint" in the days when Jesus walked among men in Palestine. What changes there are have been more in degree than in kind, for man is still man, and sin is still sin; and when these two are mixed, sin wreaks the same damaging havoc to man's life that it has always done. Samuel Shoemaker wrote in his remarkable testimony, *The Conversion of the Church,*

Just as in that day the church was born, and released a mighty surge of redeeming and cleansing power among men, just so, in our time, the untoward conditions argue that a new revelation of Christ through His Church is necessary. There is no other salvation for men. Nothing less than a God-inspired awakening, "a rushing, mighty wind" from heaven, bearing upon its wings the fire of grace from the throne of God, is sufficient for the need of the world in this hour. Thanks be to God, the wind is stirring.

. . . It appears that once more, as often before in the time of desperate human need, God Almighty is ready to refresh His Church and revive His world with a new grant of His Holy Spirit. I believe it will be utterly impossible much longer to hold back the tide of renewal.

It was from this dedicated, spirit-empowered pastor of the Protestant Episcopal Church that I learned that a world which has once known the joy and peace of the gospel of Jesus Christ will not long be content to remain morally and spiritually bankrupt when help is within reach. But whether the church as we know it, and as we have helped to make it, is in the vanguard of this awakening and is awakened by it is our particular problem. Will the church of this day be sufficiently renewed to conserve and reproduce the miracle of changed lives, by being willing to quicken our pace, to change some of our ways, to seek the deepening of our experience of vital relationship to our Lord Jesus Christ, and to throw ourselves more fully into his work of redeeming human personality? This is a question which we must answer, not by public pronouncements, but by the individual decisions of thousands of our ministers and laymen. True renewal has always come from unsuspected sources and has usually fooled the institutionalists and the intellectuals at first.

The church today must take its opportunity while it is here, or the day may well come again, as it has at times in past history, when it will be found wanting and opportunity will be lost altogether. Not that Christ's church, which he is building, would or could fail, but we, who are the human stuff out of which redeemed building material is to come for the completion of his church, may fail to be the kind of building material he can use. We need to be obedient to his will and plans and purposes so that when we represent him in the world, we serve as those who are *in* the world but not *of* it. This is our need. For the perfecting of his church, God has time—he creates time. Time serves him. But we have only our short hour compared with God's endless time. Therefore, what we are to do must be done quickly. If we choose to disobey his requirements for spiritual enduement, then God can afford to pass us by until he can raise up another generation that will not murmur against him when it comes to Kadesh-Barnea, at the threshold of the Promised Land.

I believe that any church that is putting its emphasis anywhere else than on bringing people in touch with the living God is out of date and blind alike to the danger and the unparalleled opportunity of our present day. We need a new ministry of men and women intent not upon the maintenance of institutions, but upon the transformation of lives. I do not mean this in the narrow, hackneyed sense in which such words are usually used, for I know that institutions and organizations are essential to the carrying on of the life and work of the church. I cannot accept the assertion made by some today that the day of the parish or congregation is past. Reliance on mere organization and structure is certainly not enough, but even God, when he wanted to make known his redeeming love for man, became incarnate in the structured and organized body of a man.

To indicate that this is not the new problem that some

would try to make of it, I refer to a letter written many years ago by the minister of Trinity Church in Boston which he sent to his friend, Edward Lincoln Atkinson, on his call to Epiphany Church in New York City:

We ministers are tempted to work for the salvation of parishes. It is a mistake. Our sole endeavor should be to labor for the salvation of souls (persons); that is, the upbuilding of individual lives. If the parish, as a parish, prospers, so much the better; if it does not, it is not significant. The decay of the parish is nothing; the strengthening of weak wills, the illumination of dim consciences and the inspiration of helpless people mean everything.

That is strong, but true; we shall not get a new church until we begin to believe it and to build upon this spiritual principle.

The spiritual renewal essential to the *new church* we have been considering will be accompanied by several pentecostal marks, which were evidenced in the Upper Room church and have always been present in every age in which the church of Jesus Christ became truly manifest. There are four such marks to which I briefly call attention.

First, there must be *unity*. "They were all together in one place." This is a spiritual unity, not necessarily organic. In Jerusalem, it took several days of prayer and understanding and forgiveness of one another before the barriers that separated them were broken down, the "egos" were humbled, and the will and way of the Lord Jesus Christ became all-consuming. It will take a similar experience today to produce similar results. This applies to parishes and congregations as well as to denominations.

Artificial union will not solve this problem. This requires "unity of the Spirit in the bond of peace."

Second, there must be the recognition of *the source of spiritual power*. That which happened in the Upper Room was "heaven-born" and "heaven-sent." There is a difference between man-made programs or heaven-inspired obedience. Each bears its own credentials. Too many people get lost in debate about the "sound *like* wind" and the "tongues *like* flames of fire," whereas the important truth is the source of the power of this new church. It was heaven-commissioned. We need to be sure that our reliance is not primarily on our own human wisdom and skills and experience. Our reliance must be on the Holy Spirit, who makes Christ known and endues the church through his indwelling presence in every believer. Somehow we get too much enamored with the flashy and unusual or the sensational, rather than seeking earnestly to know what God's will and purpose for his world may be. It is true that there is little glamour or honor among men for doing the regular, faithful, and plodding witnessing required in the life and work of his church. Our need is to be faithful workers.

Third, we must remember that the Upper Room church was a *witnessing church*. Its theme was: *the mighty works of God*. In this connection, it needs to be said that too many who read the account in the second chapter of Acts are sidetracked by the various tongues that are spoken. The important thing is that which they spoke about in all the tongues that were used. They did not talk about themselves or their organization or their programs; they spoke of the mighty acts of God—what God had done and was doing in Jesus Christ! As Peter summarized it that day, "God has made him both Lord and Christ."

Tongues are not an end in themselves to be sought for their own sake. They are for service. They are vehicles to make known the great purposes and works of Christ through his church. Whether in Jerusalem or Rome, in modern Africa or Japan or China, we must not forget why we use languages. The gospel must not be eclipsed by the vehicle that expresses it.

Finally, the *new church* was a *spiritually fruitful and productive church*. Several things conspired to produce the results that rapidly added to the growth of the church and to its outreach into the world, until in three centuries it had penetrated and saturated the cultures of the Mediterranean World. Having met the conditions of spiritual commitment, the younger generation believed and accepted the witnessing of their elders. One generation taught the next. Old men spoke of their memories of spiritual victories. This kindled visions in young men that led them to commitment to Christian service. In such a climate it was normal that those who were persuaded to invoke the name of the Lord should be saved. Nothing speaks so convincingly or so persuasively to the world as the changed lives of those who have genuinely believed and accepted the message of the mighty acts of God in Jesus Christ.

Several years ago I was guest preacher for Religious Emphasis days at Kansas State College at Pittsburg, Kansas. A splendid group of students and faculty members attended the two general convocations at which I spoke, and these gave rise to numerous interviews. The first day I spoke to them on the challenge of the world in revolution, with three major tension points that are in need of a worldwide solution: the race question, the question of war and peace, and the question of Christian unity. I stressed the need for men and women of Christian conviction and experience to offer themselvs for the solution of these problems. There was a general enthusiastic hearing and reception for this address, and many stayed after the session to talk about these matters.

The next day I spoke to them of the necessity for the proper spiritual preparation of the individual so that he would be equipped to go into the world to work for such solutions. I pointed out that there are many who express a great interest in these worldwide issues who have never faced the basic problem of the issues within their own lives. There is a world within, with basic problems of our humanity, that needs to be dedicated to God in order that he may work through us to reach the world without. Often, it is easier and safer to try to save the world than it is to permit ourselves first to be "saved" by the grace of God, so that he can equip us spiritually for service as a vital part of his church. Following this message, only two persons came to talk with me about it. One was the head of the English Department, who thanked me for this emphasis as a necessary complement to the challenge to world service. The other was the Roman Catholic chaplain on the campus, who said: "Bishop, I know exactly what you were speaking about, for I have experienced it in my own life. Not until we come into living encounter with Jesus Christ as our Savior and Lord do we have the resources within ourselves that will make us capable of representing the mighty acts of God throughout the world."

He was *so* right! Whenever enough of us understand this and seek this kind of spiritual renewal, we will have the *new church* in our time.